Assholes: A Field Guide

Assholes: A Field Guide

How to Deal with Difficult People At Home or at Work

Philip C. Edwards

ISBN-13: 9781547297382
ISBN-10: 1547297387
Library of Congress Control Number: 2017909360
CreateSpace Independent Publishing Platform
North Charleston, South Carolina

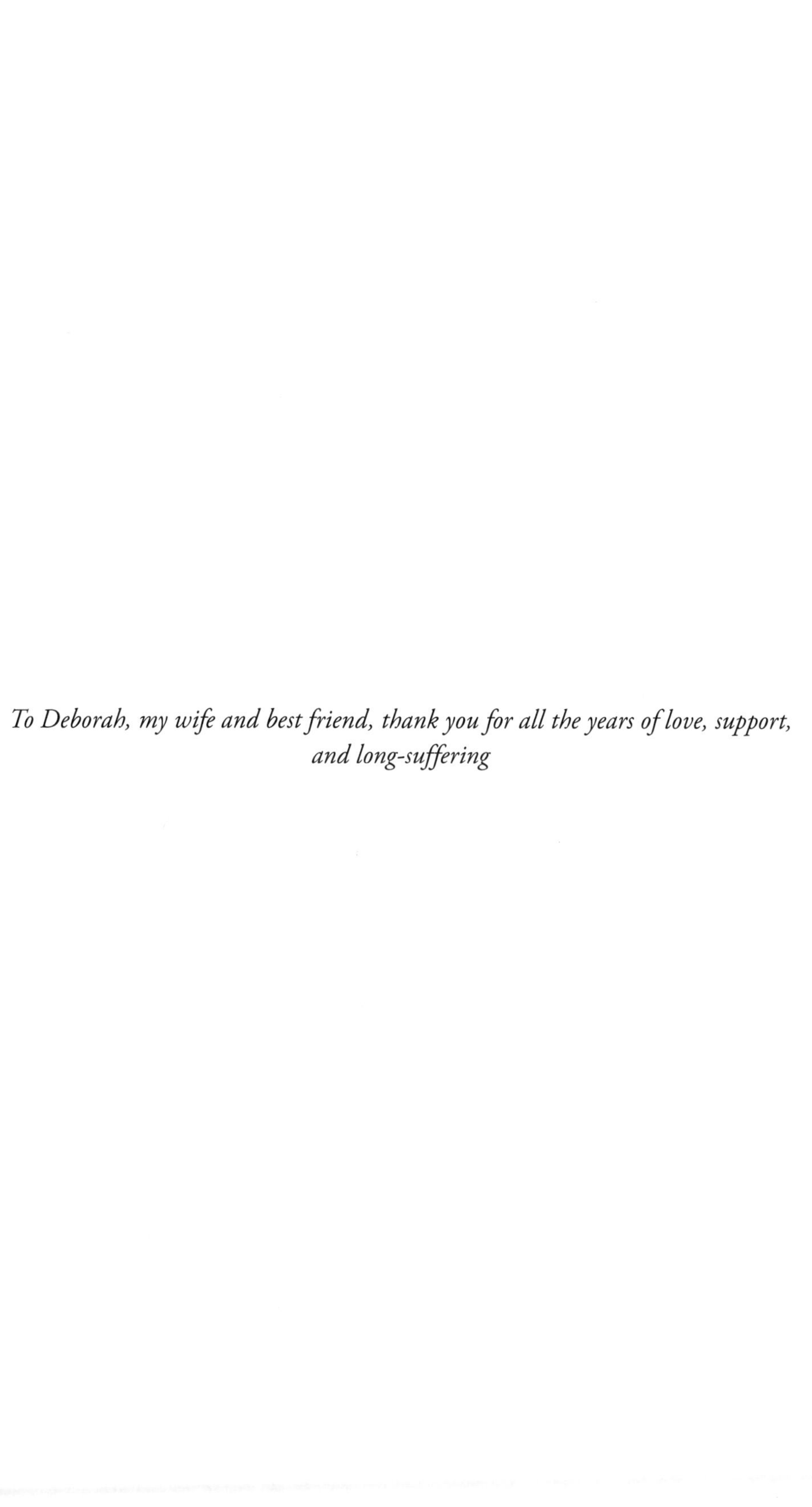

To Deborah, my wife and best friend, thank you for all the years of love, support, and long-suffering

Acknowledgments

Thank you to Deborah Edwards and Fran Kirman for their proofreading and suggestions. Thank you to all of my family members, adults and children, who have been a wonderful inspiration for me and have helped keep me on a healthy life path.

Also by Phil Edwards

See other writings by Phil on his website, chooserightly.com.
Any questions from the book, may be addressed on the website.

Gettysburg – General Lee - Nepotism

Anne Hutchinson: Trapped in Religious Freedom

Some Soldiers Stand Taller Than Others
(My Lai Massacre)

The Revolutionary War/
The Far Side of Glory

General Romeo Dallaire

Frederick Douglass

Zora Neale Hurston

It Isn't Trump

Fear on Both Sides: Israel and Palestine

Conservative Magic

Sabotaged Democracy

The Evolution of Democracy Series

Contents

Introduction

"What does your heart mean?"

A profound and puzzling question especially when it comes from a six-year old. My granddaughter, a kindergartner, Georgia Wigg, asked my wife this question when they were having a special outing at a museum in Toronto, Ontario.

My wife, perplexed at the question, asked Georgia, "What do you mean by that question?"

Georgia replied, "What your heart means is what you always do."

This conversation was in the context of how Georgia responds to the other children in her school. Out of the mouth of babes. "What does your heart mean" sets the stage for this text—a self-help book that will provide communication tools and problem-solving strategies to deal with difficult people. The purpose of the book is to understand how we personally respond to difficult people in our lives, evaluate those responses, and alter those reactions to make them more successful. The book offers time for self-reflection to understand who we are, along with case studies to evaluate different types of conflictual situations. It also provides suggestions and activity sheets to help work through how we can respond in a way that helps deescalate tense situations and provides strategies for working toward a win-win resolve.

A friend of mine recently asked me to write a book about my work with severely emotionally disturbed students. I have a multitude of interesting, funny, and informative stories from when I taught these students. Others have encouraged me to write about my Vietnam experience and pastoring in urban cities around the world. What all these different contexts have in common are people.

One day, while playing golf, the thought came to me that, in all these experiences, I have met some wonderful people of different races, ethnic origins, religions, and social and economic backgrounds. Unfortunately, the flip side of this is that I have met assholes from all these different groups. These folks, regardless of the context, were difficult to deal with and made life troublesome for those around them. At that moment on the golf course, I realized my passion was to help folks deal with difficult people and make their lives more fulfilling.

First, this is not an *us-versus-them* approach. A big part of this book is self-reflection, and a starting point is to recognize who we are. A necessary place to begin is to acknowledge that all of us have been an asshole at one time or another. One of the foundational premises of the book is to state, "We have all been assholes to some degree, but we do not have to make it a lifestyle."

Writing this book is continuing to assist me work through some of my ongoing issues, and hopefully it will help you navigate through some of yours. In each case study, if you look deep enough, you can see a bit of yourself in both the victim and the oppressor. From this vantage point, you can discover ways through the skills taught in chapter two to improve your responses and deal with others' difficult behavior.

Unfortunately dealing with others is complicated, messy, and unpredictable. No magic bullet, strategy, comment, prayer, or anything will automatically change the other person. While there are no guaranteed results for our efforts, we can learn communication skills and problem-solving strategies to help get the best results possible from conflictual situations.

When I first had the idea to write this book, I told my wife so I could solicit her thoughts. And the first words out of her mouth were, "If anyone should write a book about how to deal with assholes, it should be me, and if you do write it, don't mention me in the book. Also, if I have to proofread it, I am not going to spend my time reading the word 'asshole' on every page."

In light of her comment and the fact she has been proofreading my writing for over forty-five years, I have adopted an approach that limits the use of the word "asshole" as well as other vulgarity. In most cases, I will replace the word with the term "AH." At other times, I will use the word in order to make a specific point and have a desired effect. I have also chosen to introduce other terms in the "asshole family" even though they may not be officially recognized words in the English language. Their definitions are as they sound.

Why is there a need to limit vulgarity? Even with this new era to be vile, nasty, and mean, I want to limit the vulgarity in this work for three reasons:

1. Vulgarity is vulgar, and most people don't want to hear it all the time.
2. Vulgarity loses its effect if it is used relentlessly and flippantly. Imagine if you called everyone an AH who annoys or inconveniences you. It would get tiresome and lose its special effect.
3. Some people who need the benefit of this book may not read it if it is overwhelmed with vulgarity.

The length of this book is intentional. It comes from a lifetime of experience in working with broken people and folks who have limited time to get the help they need. For three years, I worked on a hospital ward that treated alcoholics and drug addicts. These folks were in need of help to change and better their lives. The treatment at the hospital was a twenty-one-day residential program. Even though most patients were detoxed, the attendees were nervous, unsettled, and apprehensive about their next steps. What reinforced their recovery were therapy, group, and helpful literature. The material that helped them the most were pamphlets and short, easy-to-read books that presented the rationale and tools needed to help in recovery and build better skills for daily living. The patients in their weakened physical and emotional condition could manage these books. So why read a 250-page book when you can get the same information in less than half of that? I have made this self-help book easy for you to acquire communication skills, problem-solving strategies, motivation, and encouragement to deal with difficult people.

This is not an academic approach to dealing with AHs. There will not be an endless presentation of research papers, studies done by academicians, essays written by experts, or a collection of quotes by insightful people. This is an everyday person's (not elitist) commonsense approach to identifying and dealing with assholes. At times there will be a reference from other works that will illuminate the subject, but the main resource is your common sense, thinking, and work. You are the master of your ship, and you are responsible for it.

What does your heart mean? It is what you do most of the time. It is who you are. This is an opportunity to look again at who you are, make some adjustments that improve who you are, and add skills to your tool collection that will help you deal with difficult people. Every day the choice is ours to improve ourselves, remain the same, or fall farther behind. My passion is that we find new channels to make our (and others') lives more meaningful and joyful.

It is tough being human. Occasionally, when someone is frustrated with human behavior, he or she says, "If only we could be like the animals." The thought is that creatures in nature act better than humans do. Sometimes that is true. However, a closer look at nature reveals that our human species, while not perfect, has developed a sense of civility.

As you read the cases of human interaction in this book, compare them to the animal behaviors cited at the beginning of each chapter. Sometimes our behavior is comparable to the animals. Other times we rise above our animal instincts. We can learn, and we can change.

Dung Beatle

There are several types of dung beetles. These beetles find manure, then roll and shape it, make it their home, feed off it, mate in it, lay their eggs in it, and raise their offspring in it. They say, "Home is where the heart is." Where is your heart? Where do you spend most of your time?

One

Definition and Origin

The term “asshole” (or “arsehole”) seems to have been first used in the eleventh century. Eventually it was used metaphorically to describe disgusting places on earth. Still later it was attributed to detestable people. Geoffrey Nunberg, in his book *Ascent of the A-Word*, argues that GIs in World War II adopted the term to refer to officers who were more than mere jerks. They brought the term home and popularized it for the country. Today everyone has heard the term, almost all have said the phrase, and most of us have used it repeatedly about people who have displeased us.

However, common sense suggests that the term was used much earlier. I think Neanderthals first used it. Just picture two of these hairy not-quite-human creatures hunched over outside a cave’s entrance, looking at each other after one of them has repeated the same stupid mistake for the umpteenth time. In total disbelief, the other one glares at his Neanderthal companion, points to his anus with one finger, points to his companion with the other hand, and says, “*#@!*:<> +=++_)&$%” which translates to “you asshole.”

For creationists, the story may go like this. God kicked Adam and Eve out of the Garden of Eden because they ate the forbidden fruit. Adam had been blaming Eve for all the difficulties and hardships they were now encountering because Eve had encouraged him to eat the apple. This was their first sin. Not only was ejection from the garden the consequence for this original sin but they would face tedium, toil, troubles, and hardships that would plague their lives outside the garden.

After listening to Adam blame her repeatedly for all their newfound difficulties, Eve finally said, "#%^!!+*<<"{}|/" which translates to "Not everything is my fault, asshole. Get over it."

So what does the word *asshole* (or as I will abbreviate it, AH) mean? Some of the synonyms found in various dictionaries define it using terms like "stupid," "annoying," "detestable," "entitled," "uppity," "arrogant," "insensitive," "contemptible," "vulgar," "powerful," "spoiled," "toxic," and a host of other undesirable adjectives. While not looking for a clinical definition of the term, for now, let's agree that the recipient of the term has or has not said or done something that has really upset the other person.

Criteria

Unfortunately no universally accepted formula is used to determine if a person is an AH or not. There is no AH meter or scale. Various authors have constructed their formulas based on their research, experience, vocations, and relationships.

With each formula, a person must satisfy the criteria in order to qualify as an AH. Some formulas are simple with two or three criteria, while others are more complex and demanding. Some of the qualifiers are as follows:

- The offender must have power over his or her victim.
- There must be intent.
- Someone has to be hurt or humiliated.
- Abuse of privilege, power, or position must be an element.
- The offender must feel entitled.
- There must be negative tangible or intangible effects on the recipient.
- There must be a persistent pattern of behavior.

The problem with formulas is that there are always exceptions, gray areas, or unknown circumstances. For example, we have all waited seemingly eternally in line, only to have someone cut in at the front of the line and get away with it.

A first thought is, *What an asshole.*

Maybe that person was in line previously. Perhaps he or she could have a medical reason for going to the front of the line. Or the individual worked there and was needed inside. Who knows? There could be a perfectly reasonable explanation for the action.

Developing Criteria

Here is where this book is unique and takes a turn from others. It puts the responsibility of developing criteria on you, the reader. The book will not be setting out a documented formula to define what an asshole is. That task is for you, the reader. Your formula will not be static or set in stone but will most likely change as you transform and grow. You are going to develop your own criteria using your experiences and the resources of this book.

While taking on the responsibility of creating your personal formula, there is an added responsibility to accept the consequences of and live with your decisions. Not everyone is going to agree with your criteria, and he or she doesn't have to. *You* are the one who must live with your decision. You may not be able to justify your position and feelings to satisfy others, but in your world, a person is an AH because you set the criteria. And in your world, that is correct. We actually do this every day when making decisions and judgments in our lives. We determine the criteria and the exceptions.

Is it not dangerous ground to make yourself the final determining factor in this decision? It sounds arrogant and self-serving, to a point. You may even feel like an AH for doing this. It may seem like that at first glance, but in reality, the individual has the final say in matters of his or her own life on a daily basis. You make the choice to act, to dismiss, or to participate on a daily basis. Some will be consistent with your belief system; others will not. The trick is to make good choices that will be healthy for you and others. Hopefully while reading this book, you will find suggestions and strategies for making healthy decisions and the moral fiber to live peacefully with those judgments.

With any decision you make, you live with the consequences of those verdicts and take responsibility for them. Since you have to live with your decisions, it is best in both the short and long term to make good choices based on well-thought-out criteria and principles. To do this, there is the need to develop moral principles, guidelines, strategies, and techniques that will steer you to the goal of good decision making. All of us will make mistakes. That is the simple reality of life, but we can and should avoid unforced errors in judgment.

In 1976, my wife, two daughters, and I left Bethel Theological Seminary for a year to participate in a new urban training program in Chicago called Seminary Consortium for Urban Pastoral Education (SCUPE). I was placed with a minister responsible for starting a new church on the north side of Chicago, specifically in a place called the Sunnyside Mall area in Uptown. The *Guinness Book of World Records* wrote up the local high school, Sinn, as being the most diverse high school on earth.

Just before we arrived, the police arrested more than 125 prostitutes in a single night in and around the mall area. My ministry included working with gang members, poor Appalachian whites, minorities, a vast variety of ethnic groups, homeless people, alcoholics, prostitutes, drug users, and the highest concentration of mentally ill persons in Illinois. The state had just flushed out the mental institutions and forced thousands of patients into ghetto areas like Sunnyside Mall.

I felt comfortable and capable working with all sorts of people from a variety of backgrounds. Being a Vietnam veteran added to my confidence in relating to and assisting disadvantaged and desperate people. Proverbs 16:18 says, "Pride goes before the fall," which rang loud and true in my case.

Several times a week in the area, I randomly saw a young African American man with a large, disarming smile. He was never with anyone and had an awkwardness about him. We made eye contact several times but were never in a position to say hello.

One day when I was working with a few teenagers, he walked past, and one of the kids said something derogatory, which I could not fully hear. I asked what was said and who that person was. The boys told me he was not from around there. He had taken a room in one of the cheap apartment buildings because he was attending a sex-change clinic around the corner.

I had seen and done a lot in my short life, but never had I met transgender people or thought about their issues. This was so completely out of my realm of experience, and unconsciously I made the decision to avoid this person. For the next several months, we continued to make eye contact, and once when he tried to speak to me, I shrugged off his friendly gesture. After a while, I lost contact with this person.

I knew I was wrong in my actions because I felt that gnawing uncomfortable feeling deep in my being. I lacked the courage to follow my moral and spiritual principles. This was another human being with hopes and feelings just like mine, but I made the decision to reject him solely on the basis that he was different from me.

The consequences for that decision haunt me today. Every now and then, I see his smiling face and remember that I lacked the courage and maturity to accept this person. I couldn't even bring myself to wave from a distance.

Am I an asshole for that? I don't know, but *asshole* seems to be too kind a word. Setting your own formula for whom you deem to be an AH is a serious matter and should not be taken lightly, because you live with the consequences for the rest of your life.

Criteria Myths

Most writers suggest some nonnegotiable components are needed to qualify people to be assholes. Some of these suggestions are that the AH must be persistent in the behavior, intentional in his or her motivation, or in a position of power over the other person. The AH must have a feeling of entitlement, and someone must be hurt in some way.

While these may seem entirely accurate and appropriate in formulating a definition, there are exceptions to each one. However, these exceptions don't block the construct of one's individual formula. After all, your formula is a personal one constructed by you and established by your criteria.

It is worthwhile to explain why these seemingly obvious components may or may not be included in one's construct of a definition for the AH. Some suggest that, for a person to be considered an AH, his or her behavior must be persistent and consistent. In other words, he or she must behave like an AH most of the time in most situations. What will be shown later in greater detail is that people may behave like AHs only with certain types of people or specific situations. There are men who act perfectly when they are with men or in mixed company. Yet when they are alone with women, something comes unglued, and they are demeaning, arrogant, and obnoxious. There are probably reasons for this change in character, but they act like jerks when in the company of women.

Consider the sports fan who is a quiet, normal, and reasonable person 98 percent of the time. However, when watching his or her team or child play, he or she goes bonkers and becomes obnoxious, yelling, screaming, and berating the officials and the other team. He or she is a persistent AH in these situations but acts appropriately at all other times.

Intent is a component some argue is essential for a person to be an AH. The rationale is that, if the individual didn't intend to do something assholeish, he or she is not an AH because this person did not mean to do it. Driving a motor vehicle makes AHs out of most of us because we drive aggressively, text while driving, drive overly cautious, or react to reckless drivers by yelling at them. We drive or react in a way that distracts our attention, which is not safe and makes others and us vulnerable. There is no intent to do harm to anyone, but our assholeish behavior puts others and ourselves in jeopardy.

For example, people who run yellow lights mean no harm. They certainly do not intend to cause a traffic accident. They believe they are not breaking the law. So no harm, no foul. In their minds, they are justified to run through yellow lights. They reject the principle that the yellow light is a warning and caution for the motorist to slow down and stop in order to have a clear intersection and avoid traffic mishaps. They believe they are being cautious when they roll through the yellow light because they look both ways. Their intent is not to hurt or cause harm. Nevertheless they are AHs in many folks' eyes because they habitually and continually put motorists in potential danger even though that is not their intent.

It is suggested that the AH must be in a position of power or rank over another person in order to enter the AH fold. These situations are found in places of work, the military, clubs, or organizations with a well-defined chain of command. Many employees often refer to their bosses as AHs. Almost everyone coming through the ranks has encountered a boss or supervisor who is more than a pain in the rear, he or she is a real asshole. When the underlings huddle together and complain about the boss, they can also readily identify the AHs among themselves, those fellow employees who do not do their share; complain about everyone, everything, and anything; sabotage deadlines; and act just like the boss. Being an AH is not limited to the powerful, rich, or well positioned. Assholeishness is not discriminatory. It crosses political, social, economic, educational, regional, and national boundaries. We all have an equal shot at it. It is an equal opportunity employer.

Entitlement crosses all classes and boundaries as well. You don't have to be powerful or well-heeled to feel entitled. All you have to do is think you are better than someone else is. In your mind, you are justified to treat others poorly, that is, belittle, neglect, and abuse them.

One needs to look no further than a poor family in which one member acts in a dysfunctional manner and the other family members resent him or her. The dysfunctional member looks after his or her needs at the expense of the other family members. The person may feel he or she has more potential, is smarter and better in tune, and believes his or her needs are more critical than those of the others. This is a real AH even though he or she is poor. On the playground, the child left out of games may feel he or she is justified in treating others poorly the way AHs do. To be an AH, you only have to act like an AH. Behavior is the determining factor.

The final myth buster is the notion that someone always gets hurt and feels pain by the AH's action or behavior. Usually this is the case, and a person does get hurt, either physically, mentally, emotionally, spiritually, or economically. There are exceptions.

A young mother in my church worked for a large company in Toronto, Ontario. Under her were two sisters who were both going to university and earning money to help pay for their schooling. My young parishioner reported that these two young women were mischievous but excellent, hardworking women. Many working there considered one of the business partners as a real asshole. He would belittle them in front of others, raise his voice, swear at them, blame them for things he had told them to do, and use them as excuses for why things did not succeed. When visitors came, he would ask the guest in front of his employee if he or she knew of any responsible, qualified person to do this job.

One day he was especially rude and demeaning to one of the sisters. While working in the mailroom, one sister came across his application for some periodicals he had put in the outgoing mail. She checked off and added several women's magazines. The sisters smiled as they considered how he would be inconvenienced by rectifying this situation with all the calls and letters to cancel the unwanted subscriptions. Was the CEO hurt or just inconvenienced?

An acquaintance of mine was known to be a cheapskate. While on a cruise with other friends, he had an almost full bottle of rum opened. The crew instructed him that he could not disembark from the ship with the open bottle of liquor. Instead of leaving it for the crew, which his other friends had done with their open bottles, he tried to finish it the night before, even though he was not particularly fond of rum. He finished the rum before disembarking. The crew was obviously unaware of his actions, and to their knowledge his stinginess did not hurt them. However, he came through with flying asshole colors.

Criteria Questions

Most of us reject labeling children as AHs. Take a child under six who takes his or her younger siblings' toys and breaks them repeatedly. The child is loved, cared for, and disciplined for his or her behavior. No matter how much attention is given to this bad behavior, it continues. When the six-year-old goes to kindergarten, he or she breaks other children's toys and is disciplined. Knowing the history of the child, a staff worker says, "What a little asshole."

Is the six-year-old an AH? Yes or no? For the staff worker, yes is correct because he is looking at behavior and he has set this as his definition. Some may want to qualify calling the child an AH until they discover why the child breaks others' toys. Is it something he has learned or some defect within that can't be controlled?

To the staffer, it does not make a difference. The child is an AH because of his or her behavior, regardless of age or cause. The staffer may not have the resources or expertise to clinically diagnose the child, just as we don't have the time, resources, expertise, opportunity, or inclination to determine the root cause for the bad behavior of adult assholes in our lives. It could be a predominance of nature or nurture or an equal combination of the two. This does not alter the opinion of the observer.

Whether the cause is nature or nurture, it does not make a difference when dealing with behavior. What will make a distinction is the person's relationship with the child, knowledge of the youngster, and one's temperament at that moment.

For fifteen years, I taught ESE (Exceptional Student Education) students in public schools. These students were diagnosed as "severely emotionally disturbed," and all were on at least one form of medication. They all had a clinical reason to act in inappropriate ways at times. Just because they had a clinical reason for acting up did not mean that, as teachers, we accepted their inappropriate behavior. On the contrary, our job as teachers was to monitor and manage that behavior in order to help them and keep the other students safe. Our ultimate goal was to help the students manage their own behavior in order to successfully function and interact with others.

As teachers, adults, parents, and neighbors in a community, we are forced to deal with others' behaviors every day. We may not understand it, but we must deal with it. Some of that behavior is asshole behavior, and we are justified in making those kind of judgments on our own, guided by our own judgment and common sense.

Messy Work

Working with people can be complicated, but it is not rocket science, mathematical, or predictable. And it is not governed by a rigid set of rules that works for everyone every time. Working with people is messy, and you will get dirty. In light of this reality, everyone can learn strategies and techniques to deal with these situations. The title of this book is *Assholes: A Field Guide*. I have based this book on the reality that common ordinary folks can learn to identify and manage the assholes in their lives.

It can be confusing trying to figure people out and know how to relate to them! The following is an article I wrote that was published in our local community paper in December 2016 that demonstrates how conflicted one can be when working with others.

Democracy Challenged

Have you ever loved and hated someone at the same time? It's complicated. I grew up with Daniel Boone and Davey Crocket being my boyhood heroes. Soon Andrew Jackson was added to that list as a result of listening to Johnny Horton's song, "The Battle of New Orleans." After studying the battle, I realized just how remarkable it was that America won that battle. Jackson, outnumbered, faced off against the best-trained and equipped army in the world with backwoodsmen, militia, ragtag volunteers, Indians, pirates, and an uncooperative New Orleans population. My admiration grew when I learned he defended his wife's honor and took a bullet during a duel that affected him for the remainder of his life.

Jackson served as president from 1829–1837. "Ole Hickory" in the White House—what could go wrong with an iron-willed, tougher-than-nails former Indian fighter making decisions about how the whole country should run? Jackson used Native Americans when it benefited him, but he really did not like them. Those feelings translated to a belief that Native Americans and whites could not live together peacefully, and he set out to create a national policy that would separate natives from whites. In 1830 he signed the Indian Removal Act that displaced natives from Michigan to Florida from their homes and put them on reservations in Oklahoma.

The Cherokee in Tennessee and Georgia challenged this by taking their case to the Supreme Court of the United States. *They won* and were now able to stay in their homes on the land their ancestors had occupied for thousands of years. They had developed towns, national and local governments, and English-speaking schools that outperformed those of the white communities. They had assimilated fully into America culture, except for the color of their skin.

That assimilation did not satisfy Jackson. He said the court could make any decision it wanted to make but challenged the court to enforce it. He then ordered the army to forcefully remove all natives east of the Mississippi to reservations in Oklahoma. In mid-November, as the cold and snow set in, natives were rounded up with no warning or opportunity to gather things for the trip or the weather conditions. The old, young, sick, weak, pregnant, and others were herded onto wagons, taken to holding areas, and then forced to march west. Over four thousand died: parents watched their children perish, youngsters watched as parents were buried in shallow graves along the roadside, and grandparents too weak to walk or withstand the conditions gave up their spirit. The journey became known as the Trail of Tears.

After I learned this, my hero, Andrew Jackson, went from being a patriotic war hero to a murderer of thousands of innocents. By disregarding the verdict of the Supreme Court, Jackson challenged the very structure of the Constitution and made himself the supreme authority. If he had continued in this manner and other presidents followed his suit, there would be no democracy known as the United States of America.

Love and Hate. I love Jackson because he was a determined man of action who loved and cared for his wife. I hate Jackson because he used people when he needed them and then discarded them. He hated those who were racially different and orchestrated their death through his racist policies. What do you do when you love and hate someone or something in the same breath? You do the best you can. No easy answers. Working with people is messy.

Myotonic Goats

These goats are referred to as "fainting goats" or "stiff-legged goats." When this breed of goat gets nervous, startled, or frightened, their muscles tense up, and they fall over paralyzed for several minutes. Imagine if this happened to humans, and we fell over paralyzed every time we got nervous or anxious. This would be particularly troublesome if we were driving. We are fortunate to be able to learn skills that help us work through our anxiety. We do not have to be slaves to our emotions.

Two

Communication Skills and Problem-Solving Strategies

Communication and negotiation skills are the first line of defense and a beginning offense for managing assholes. Learning skills to communicate and negotiate with individuals and groups will be your toolset kept in your back pocket whenever you need it. These skills will help us from behaving like myotonic goats and just falling over paralyzed. While there is no magical tool for success, you don't need to go into a situation feeling defenseless and overpowered or crazed with anger, throwing verbal hand grenades and having guns blazing. You can develop a set of tools that can help you work through the most difficult situations.

For over forty-two years, I have been a member of Alcoholics Anonymous and thankfully have not taken drugs or alcohol for more than forty-five years. I am still in a state of recovery, working daily on my sobriety. I have based this book on several basic premises:

1. This first belief I adopted from AA, "If you have a breath, you have hope."
2. Always leave a door open that can help the other person or your relationship. What is absolutely critical in this step is that you set the

boundaries and are in control of how you will help the person requesting assistance.

3. Treat others with respect even in the midst of the most difficult conflict. No matter how despicable the other person is behaving, it pays off in the long run to treat him or her with respect. I have seen this work in every possible situation, especially if litigation is involved.

In one of my pastorates, our family lived right downtown next to the church. The former occupant, my predecessor, welcomed visitors at his door and attempted to address their wants and needs. He was an elderly clergyman who lived there with his wife. My situation was different because I had my wife and three small children at home. Many nights I was away at meetings.

For the first six months, I would have several visitors a week at my door after hours asking for help. Most of these were men looking for money, shelter, or food. A short distance from my home was a detox center that provided shelter for the night, food, and an AA program. Because of my AA background and sensitivity to their need, I would offer to drive them to the center and get them established for the night.

My offer was refused more often than not. Some of these men just wanted money. Others wanted to spend the night in my home. A few wanted a meal. I informed them that I would be happy to help them with the shelter and food by taking them to the center. I let them know that I was always wanting to help them, but this was how I was going to meet their request. Even though my door was open to these folks, most of the time, the help was refused.

Another principle in AA is jokingly referred to as "two-by-four communication." This involves a person getting a two-by-four piece of wood, knocking it alongside a person's head to get his or her attention so a meaningful discussion can take place. Alcoholics tend to have a hard time listening and paying attention, so they need some encouragement. Rather than using a two-by-four to get someone's attention, the suggestion is to learn communication skills that will help you deal with difficult people.

Growing up in a rather dysfunctional family, our conflict-resolution style was win or lose. When in conflict our family had a winner and a loser. Things were not discussed with mutual resolve in mind. My father, a very aggressive person, forced his will on the rest of the family. My mother, on the other hand, was extremely passive. For the most part, my mother and my siblings lost. My father, like his father before him, had limited skills in working through conflicts with others. My military experience reinforced this win-lose style of communication.

Shortly after returning from Vietnam, I met the woman who later became my wife, and we now have forty-five years together. This win-or-lose communication style did not go well with her. Soon after we were married, we got into a discussion that turned into a major argument. In order to make my point, I said some things in a forceful and harsh manner.

My wife teared up and then hugged me. She said, “I don’t feel like you love me.”

I never had been hugged during an argument. On the contrary, I was hit several times but never hugged. This hug felt really strange and humbling. I didn’t know much, but I knew enough not to say anything and realized my position on the argument was not important at this time.

After this, I learned there were other ways to communicate that would not make people cry or feel bad about themselves. I began to realize there could be a resolution that satisfied everyone if people communicated differently. Though I didn’t have a framework or definition for these aptitudes at the time, I began to learn and use other communication skills that contributed to a more pleasant and happy home life.

Later after we graduated from university, I had the opportunity to take communication, conflict management, and negotiation workshops. I became a trainer and facilitator in these areas. Learning communication skills and conflict-management techniques helped me work toward win-win solutions for both parties. These skills continued to enhance my marriage and improve my relationships with others.

Communication skills and other techniques for relating with people are especially helpful when working with assholes. Here is the good and bad news for using communication skills and problem-solving strategies. The good news is that these skills work toward building relationships, clearing up misunderstandings, and resolving conflicts that can satisfy both parties. The bad news is nothing is guaranteed. Two people or parties working together are needed for the best outcome. In other words, no magic bullet, strategy, prayer, phrase, or approach can guarantee a successful conclusion. Working with people is unpredictable and can be messy; however, we should always give ourselves the best opportunity to succeed.

The following are communication skills and problem-solving techniques. If you are not familiar with them, please take the time to learn to use them. However, if you are familiar with them, feel free to review them and move onto chapter three.

Skills for Managing AHs

Tools for Conflict Management

Conflict is a natural part of life that impacts every person, group, and organization. Conflict can be a dynamic catalyst for positive change. If managed well, conflict can release new understandings, creative ideas, fresh directions, increased productivity, and strengthened relationships.

It is an opportunity to connect at a deeper level. However, mismanaged conflict can lead to hurt feelings, hostility, strained and broken relationships, and the loss of direction, time, or productivity.

Five Options to Deal with Conflict

Researchers and theorists have identified five ways of dealing with conflict, whether the skirmish is between individuals or organizations. The five ways of dealing with conflict are fight, flee, negotiate, mediate, and litigate.

If one chooses to fight, it is an arena in which parties engage in a verbal slugfest or shouting match in which one or both parties try to exert his or her will over the other without regard for the other's needs or interests. The opponent's position and arguments are not accepted, no matter how rational or accurate they may be. Listening only occurs in order to discover a weakness in the other's position and is not an attempt to understand. This is seen as a revolving-door argument. The contestants just keep repeating the same thing over and over until they get what they want on their terms. The principle strategy is to overpower the other.

Fleeing is just the opposite. One or both parties ignore, avoid, or deny the conflict. The principle characteristic is disengagement. This occurs both in personal relationships as well as in the business sector. In order to avoid a conflict or hard feelings, one party gives into the other without his or her needs being recognized or met.

Negotiation is where one or both parties acting in good faith seek to reach an agreement or understanding based on the strength of their argument or position. The principle characteristic is persuasion. The purpose of listening is to understand the other's position and seek a common resolve.

Some disputants use a third party to help them mediate their issues. The principle characteristic is working together for a mutual resolve through an objective, trusted third-party facilitator. An offshoot of this principle is to have another person on the scene when the discussion occurs to act as a support. This support person has no power or authority in the conflict but is there to help the meeting take place.

Finally, some parties look to a third party to adjudicate their case, which is litigation. The principle characteristic is relinquishing the decision making to a third party for judgment. This involves arbitrators, lawyers, and judges and naturally is also the most expensive.

Five Communication Categories

Authors of communication styles also identify five distinct categories of communication for which people have a particular preference. These categories are authoritative, submissive, accommodating, compromise, and collaboration. Various authors and theorists use different terminology to identify each of the following styles. *What is important and should never be forgotten is that every one of these styles is appropriate in the suitable context.* The first challenge is to learn to use all the styles even if you are not comfortable with a particular method. The second challenge is to use the appropriate style in the appropriate context.

The first style is "authoritative." It may also be called "assertive," "forcing," or "commanding." In a theater that has caught on fire, the manager may run into the theater and order all the attendees out of the building in a hopefully orderly fashion. A teacher raises her voice at a student to stop hitting another student. A guide on a wilderness trip tells everyone not to drink the water because it is contaminated. A boss orders a report due by tomorrow's deadline to be on his desk by one o'clock. These are all commands and are quite appropriately used in these contexts.

The opposite style of authoritarian is submissive. Other terms used for this approach are "fleeing," "yielding," "capitulating," or "giving in." "Fleeing" or "giving in" seems like a cowardly option to choose, unless you have no investment in the conflict or it is simply none of your business. In this case, where the outcome means nothing to you, it is the wise decision not to get involved. People have the right and need to work out their own issues without involving themselves in others' problems unnecessarily.

The third communication style is "accommodating." In this situation, a person is involved to some degree, but the outcome has little impact on him or her. In other words, he or she really doesn't care what happens. In order to settle the matter and move on, one person is giving the other individual what he or she wants. A fellow worker needs the company car for Wednesday morning even though you are scheduled to use it. You easily have other means of transportation or could stay in the office and work on other projects. So you yield your right to the car and allow the coworker to use it. Why take time and energy to fight about it or be uncooperative? Why be an asshole?

Compromise is a category that satisfies both parties partially. It is a helpful option to get the process moving in a positive way and to get people to work together. Finding a bit of common ground provides the opportunity for working through bigger issues together later. Each party gives a little bit to get a little bit, that is, "I will do this for you if you do this for me."

The last category is collaboration, the highest level of communication. Collaboration seeks to satisfy the needs of both parties fully. Each party is listening to the other's position for understanding and attempting to discover ways to meet the needs that are revealed. Both parties work together to find creative solutions that will satisfy them both. This strategy and endeavor usually produces the strongest and most lasting resolves because everyone has his or her needs met. Working out of a collaborative framework builds relationships and strengthens bonds between people. Questions that both parties ask are, How will this affect you? What might the results be? Why is this important to you? Is there a substitute that will meet the need if this can't be acquired?

Problem-Solving Procedure

What does a problem-solving procedure have to do with managing assholes? Groups are a part of almost every aspect of our lives. They are present in our places of worship, schools, neighborhoods, condo associations, clubs, places of work, and political structures, to mention a few. Unfortunately assholes are in all those groups. Yes, even our places of worship.

After pastoring three churches for twenty years and being a part of countless church and denominational meetings, I can testify with no hesitation that assholes are present and accounted for in the faith community. They are everywhere.

One afternoon, I was in a monthly meeting with other ministers. A fellow minister's church failed, and it was closing its doors. There was a great deal of discussion about how this happened, and someone raised the question if we shared any responsibility in this church's failure. Every one of the ministers in that meeting had met numerous times with the pastor and church to help them in their need. Our local association of seventy city churches and our denomination had reached out over the years to help in a variety of ways. Even with all this assistance and input, the church failed.

One of our minsters thought we could have done more and should offer a public apology to the pastor, the church, and the association. Several argued this did not reflect the reality of the situation and an apology of any kind was not appropriate. It was suggested we share our condolences and offer help in any way the church deemed necessary.

Normally our group reaches consensus, but this one fellow clergy demanded to have his way. From this point on, we were accused of not helping and subjected to name-calling. I sat listening to these accusations, feeling angrier and angrier as the discussion continued. It bothered me that we were being asked to confess to something we had not done. I was squeezing a hot cup of coffee so hard it broke in my hand. After this minor distraction and more discussion, the group agreed to a private meeting with our fellow clergy whose church failed and anyone could share what was on his or her heart.

So it is useful to understand how groups work and how to manage those who disrupt those meetings and lead them in a negative direction. The following problem-solving procedure is something most organizations have adopted in one form or another for conducting their meetings. If your group does not follow this procedure or a like methodology, it is suggested you adopt this method to conduct meetings. Try to find a qualified person who is capable of conducting this type of meeting. It takes some practice, skill, and patience, but it can be done, and it is so rewarding. The following is a six-step problem-solving procedure:

1. Define the problem: Define the problem in one short sentence. As a participant, these are some questions to ask in getting started or if the meeting goes off track: What exactly are we trying to solve today? Can that be put in one short sentence? In a brief sentence, what is the main thing we are trying to accomplish today? Because I am unclear as to our purpose, what are we attempting to address? Because a number of ideas have been shared so far, which one are we working on now?
2. Brainstorm possible solutions: Have one person act as a recorder to list all the suggestions given by the participants to solve the problem. During this step, it is absolutely critical that *no* evaluation or *negative* comments be made about any suggestion, regardless of how ridiculous it may seem. List all suggestions. Verbally encourage participants to offer ideas. If a negative comment is made about a suggestion, remind the group that evaluations of all the offerings will be done later, but no comments about suggestions will be made now. Continue to ask for

more ideas. If the recorder fails to list a suggestion, bring it to his or her attention and have it recorded. Normally this is an oversight. If a facilitator attempts to steer the agenda by only listing suggestions that support his or her solution, this needs to be addressed immediately.

3. Evaluate each suggestion: Once all the suggestions have been made and recorded, take each idea separately and list its advantages and disadvantages. This will take some time, but it is worth it because no one will feel left out or unimportant. This is the place where other creative ideas can emerge. Dismiss suggestions if there is a consensus from the group.
4. Select a group solution by consensus or vote. Write it out so all can see.
5. Delegate responsibilities: Have different members of the group accept responsibilities for various tasks that need to be done in order to complete the objective.
6. Follow up: This will involve evaluation as the effort continues. There may be a need to reconvene in order to adjust tasks or redefine the problem.

Communication Skills

For a number of years, I taught communication skills both in churches and in local community centers. After the seminars in both places, some participants would tell me how wonderful the skills worked, while others would share their failures.

To address this situation, I invited everyone to attend one evening session a month after the seminars, at which time failures were shared. In these additional workshops, we role-played the failed situations to sort out the skills and help boost people's confidence and ability to use the skills.

Skill building is not an easy matter, and it is difficult to acquire and develop skills from just a book. Workshops and seminars are offered in almost every community in the country. Some of these are free, while others will charge a fee. It is well worth the investment to enroll in communication skills seminars or workshops to develop and practice newly acquired skills.

Active Listening Skills

The first set of communication skills is called active listening skills. One of the most meaningful experiences a person can have is to know he or she has been heard and understood in a conversation. It is a way of validating you as a speaker and valuing you as a person. Active listening skills provide the listener with both verbal and nonverbal abilities on how to listen and demonstrate to the speaker that he or she has been heard and understood.

When I first started working with severely emotionally disturbed students, I had to write a case study on a student. I was assigned an autistic student and had to interview his family and him. The mother provided background history on her family and the impact her autistic son had on the family. She and her husband had three sons prior to their autistic child. She knew something was different with him because he acted unlike her other three boys at an early age. One of the most noticeable behaviors was this youngest child did not like to be touched or held. People kept telling her things would be fine and he just needed time to grow out of some of his behaviors.

I asked her what her most memorable moment was in bringing up her son. She said, before he was diagnosed with autism, the actions of her youngest made her feel confused and frightened. He would throw tantrums and have outbursts, and nothing seemed to console him.

One day she was in the meat store picking up an order of meat for a barbecue that evening. While giving the clerk her order, her son had a tantrum. It was loud and embarrassing. Other customers moved away and gave her son plenty of room as he thrashed around on the floor. The owner of the store came from the back of the store into the reception area to see what the commotion was about.

He looked at the mother and her son and then asked, "Do you have everything you came for?"

She said yes. She was trying to manage her grocery sacks and her son out the door.

The owner took her parcels and said, "I know it is difficult. We had the same problem with our son. You are doing a great job. Hang in there."

The mother told me she got home, parked the car in the driveway, and just sat there and cried and cried. Then she said, "This was the first time someone understood me."

Her life with her autistic son continued to have many bad moments, but she felt affirmed as a mother and a person because at least one other person understood her.

Active listening is listening to understand, not just to hear. It involves paying attention with all your receptors. The first step in active listening is to make sure all your electronic devices are shut off and put away. Next make sure to stop talking, look at the speaker, give gestures to show the speaker you are listening, sit or stand up straight, and give welcoming facial expressions such as a smile. These let the speaker know that you are listening.

Verbal statements can also let the speaker know you have heard and understood or are trying to comprehend his or her message. Some responses that help are as follows:

- "Could you repeat that?"
- "I am not sure what you mean by that."
- "It is unclear to me how that relates to what you just said."
- "Let me make sure I understand you."
- "Tell me if this is correct or if I have misunderstood you."
- "Let me see if I can repeat back to you in my words what you just said."
- "Tell me if I missed something or added something you did not say."

Statements like these let the speaker know you understand or are trying to comprehend. It will also prevent misunderstanding, which can get the discussion off track or end up in the revolving door syndrome.

One can make certain errors in responding to a speaker that can derail or shut down a discussion. Interrupting and finishing what you think the speaker is saying is demoralizing. Other errors are showing too much or not enough emotion, minimizing his or her concern, adding to his or her comments, omitting part of the comment, acting like a therapist and diagnosing the speaker, not keeping up with the speaker, or completely changing the subject. All these injections hinder good communication among people.

Assertive Skills

After learning how to listen, there is an equally important need to learn how to speak to others. This section will focus on positive assertive skills. Unfortunately there are numerous negative assertive techniques such as bullying, talking over someone, using sarcasm, yelling, interrupting, blaming, and others. The use of negative confrontational approaches blocks or completely stops dialogue and will make reaching a healthy outcome almost impossible.

Positive assertive communication allows the speaker to speak up on his or her own behalf. It gives the speaker the opportunity to share his or her concern in an honest and forthright manner while respecting and valuing the other person. One of the greatest benefits of this approach is that it establishes the value of the speaker as a person. It builds up his or her self-esteem and communicates to others that the speaker and his or her input is valuable. Other advantages to this approach are the speaker's needs are shared, he or she is affirmed, it clears the air, and it builds honest relationships.

A popular and excellent confrontation skill is called "I messages." This skill assists the speaker in communicating the problem, sharing his or her feelings, and explaining the negative effects on the speaker of the other person's behavior. The hopeful result is that the listener will see how his or her behavior is hurting the speaker and then correct the behavior so as not to do more damage.

An "I message" can have three or four parts. Elements of the three-part "I message" are a nonjudgmental statement of the negative behavior of the other person; the speaker's feelings about the behavior; and the negative effect the behavior is having on the speaker. The four-part "I message" adds the element of consequences. Both the three- and four-part "I message" have their advantages.

A necessary component of the *negative-effect statement* is that it is given with no judgments or blaming descriptors. It is a clear statement of the behavior, highlighting what the listener is doing that is affecting the speaker in a negative manner. "I messages" require the offending person to be identified ("When you raise your voice…") and their action clearly stated.

A judgment example is, "You really *lowered yourself* when you said my idea was useless. It hurt my feelings and made me hesitant to share anymore." A nonjudgmental "I message" is, "You really hurt my feelings when you said my idea was useless. That kept me from sharing in the group as much as I wanted to." With the "I message," the speaker is not making a moral or character judgment about the other person. Rather the speaker is merely identifying the person who did the offending action.

BATNA

Roger Fisher and William Ury coined the term "best alternative to a negotiated agreement (BATNA)" to refer to a situation in bargaining in which a person might not get all he or she wants. BATNA simply is what a person will settle for. Nations prepared to go to war, corporations with millions of dollars at stake, spouses considering divorce, or friends in conflict can use this action plan. Basically an individual goes into a negotiation with certain expectations, but if things don't go well, BATNA is what the person will accept. A follow-up consideration is to decide what consequences are acceptable. Another deciding factor is always the individual's relationship with the other person and the end consequences. Will the outcome of the negotiation change the relationship, and is that change acceptable?

During the election of 2016, the country was exposed to an excellent but shocking example of BATNA being played out on the national stage before the whole world. The Democratic campaign aired a video of Andrew Tesoro's architectural firm that designed the Trump National Golf Club in Westchester, New York. Andrew Tesoro claimed he sent a bill to Trump that was not paid. He had a meeting with Trump and was offered less than one-third of what he was owed. Still the bill was not paid. When that bill was not paid, another meeting was set, and Tesoro was told he could fight the nonpayment, but it would take him years to collect, and ultimately he would go broke. He was offered even less this time but felt he had to accept the offer because of his firm's vulnerability.

In any BATNA situation, the party must decide what he or she is willing to accept. Sometimes the person can hold out and challenge the other party. In the case of Mr. Tesoro, he had bills to pay and other responsibilities to meet. He felt forced to settle, even though he may have felt he was being bullied and cheated. However, he weighed his BATNA and made his decision to settle whether it was fair or not.

All of these skills are used to assist in managing assholes and others. Naturally they are not all used in every situation. They are your tools to learn, practice, and use in an effective, appropriate manner. Using these skills will help define your relationships and your life.

Blue Heron

The great blue heron is usually seen standing elegantly alone by the side of a lake, stoically contemplating life or watching for a meal. Though much smaller, bands of crows attack blue herons. Ornithologists refer to this action as mobbing. *They believe crows do this to protect nests and establish territory. Many of the majestic blue herons are killed as a result of mobbing. Humans have developed ways to settle land disputes and protect their property without the need to destroy others. We have learned to share and resolve conflict peacefully.*

Three

Sacred Cow Asshole (SCAH)

Types of Assholes (AHs)

AHs come in all different sizes, shapes, genders, races, intellectual capabilities, and economic levels, and they display different temperaments, personalities, degrees of sophistication, and any other differences one can imagine. The remainder of the book will do primarily two things:

1. To identify nine different types of AHs in broad strokes: the Sacred Cow AH, the Boss AH, the Bigoted AH, the Events AH, the Knee-Jerk AH, the Tech AH, the Awkward AH, the Consummate AH, and the Exceptional AH
2. To provide suggestions on how to survive and manage these different types of AHs

Sacred Cow Asshole (SCAH)

Now we enter dangerous waters, where whatever is said will most likely offend someone. This is the corral of sacred cows. There are as many sacred cow issues as there are people; however, only five major types will be highlighted. Sacred cows will be discussed in the context of religion, race, patriotism, business, and contemporary issues. Their devotees passionately hold these issues and positions presented, and one runs the risk of being ostracized for broaching these topics or questioning their positions.

By bringing up the following subjects, no disrespect is intended in any form. On the contrary, these issues are extremely important and need to be addressed despite the danger of harsh response by closed-mindedness and rabid devotees who refuse to deal with their sacred cow issues objectively.

There are two purposes for this chapter:

1. To provide strategies and tools for dealing with sacred cow assholes (SCAHs)
2. To offer hope that SCAHs will see the light and bend just a little bit to enter a reasonable dialogue, without resorting to name-calling and attacking those who raise honest and sincere questions

What is a sacred cow? Throughout the history of humankind, different religions, ethnic groups, races, and civilizations have worshiped animals. Today Hindus, more than any other religious group, revere some animals as sacred. And the most revered animal in Hinduism is the cow. While millions may go hungry throughout India, cows wander through the streets of villages and cities without being harmed or used for food because they are considered sacred and are protected by the government and populace alike. Hence, they are "sacred cows."

Westerners now label such issues as sacred cows when beliefs are held so passionately that they don't make rational sense to others. Not eating cows for religious reasons seems irrational to those in Western civilizations, where there is not a reverence for animals. However, these "newer, more advanced Western countries" with their monotheistic religions have created their own sacred cows in the forms of holy books, institutions of government, laws, economic systems, rights and freedoms, morals, and faith issues.

One example of this is how monotheistic religions treat their holy books. After returning from Vietnam, I became a Christian. This experience turned my life around, giving me a positive focus and direction. I was thrilled with the transformation in my life and desired to conform and please those in the faith. It did not take long for me to realize though that there are some real assholes in the faith community.

One weekend afternoon, I attended a presentation by a visiting speaker in our church, who was using a slide projector for his presentation. The projector needed to be raised up so the picture would fit on the screen. Trying to be helpful, I took a book and put it under the projector to raise it up. It was perfect. Problem solved. Or so I thought.

The presenter began yelling at me in front of the whole group for using a Bible to lift up the projector. He continued to yell at me, telling me this was no way to treat the Word of God. "Where is your respect for the Bible?" He yanked the Bible from under the projector, put it on a table, and replaced it with a hymnal.

Christians refer to the Bible as the Holy Bible. It is considered sacred, but not in the way this gentleman believed it to be. This was an unholy approach to a holy concept. My respect for the Bible and other religious books of faith holds a high priority in my life and deserves special respect and consideration. But to react so harshly to another person because he violated your personal sensitivity is wrong and damaging.

Unfortunately I experienced the same destructive harshness as a volunteer of the youth group for our church. The yearly denominational meeting of all our churches was held close to our location. This was to be a fun time of meeting other adolescents, enjoying youth activities, participating in nightly sing-alongs, and being away from home for the weekend.

Many of our church members attended, and we made a special effort to invite our youth and some newcomers who had just started to attend. Our kids were really enjoying the weekend away from their parents, and they enjoyed all the youth activities at the meeting.

On the second day, I was leading our youth into a sanctuary for a time of special music and singing. Just before we entered the sanctuary, a middle-aged man dressed in a coat and tie confronted us. It was the middle of the afternoon on a hot summer's day. The man began to ridicule our youth for entering the sanctuary wearing shorts and jeans.

This person's anger and aggression shocked us all, for we had been in the sanctuary the day before, wearing the same type of clothing. I tried to explain this to the gentleman, but he ranted about how we were on slippery slope, that is, allowing our youth not to respect the worship area by wearing shorts and jeans.

Fortunately one of our senior deacons was present and gently took the man off to the side for a quiet talk. One young girl was especially traumatized, but it turned out to be a good learning experience for our kids. They enjoyed the rest of meeting.

My grandfather on my mother's side was Irish. He did not drink, swear, or raise his voice. He was one of the gentlest persons I have ever known. My grandfather was slight of build with a smile on his face all the time. I never knew my grandmother, but she had a reputation for being just the opposite of my grandfather. He served in World War I driving a tank. His tank was hit. He was gassed and left for dead. The doctors felt he had little chance of recuperating, so they sent him home. He loved his country and regretted not being able to continue the fight.

We made the drive from Missouri to Massachusetts every three years or so to visit my grandfather. He lived on the outskirts of town and had birch trees growing in his backyard. These seemed like enchanted trees with their white bark. My grandfather took us to Boston Harbor to see the ships and bought my brothers and me model ships to build. He was the kindest and the gentlest of men.

One day he asked me what I thought this statement meant, "Your country right or wrong."

I said, "I think it means your country could be right or it could be wrong."

It was the first time I ever saw anger on his face. He snarled and said, "Your country right or wrong is your country, and it is always right. It is your country and always will be your country."

I was afraid of him at that moment. Even at a young age, I knew my grandfather was wrong. Now I understand question and his reaction. His sacred cow was his country. In his mind, it could do no wrong, no matter what it did.

Devotees of sacred cows make themselves especially receptive to being AHs, if they can't see beyond themselves in this arena. SCAHs are not restricted to religious organizations only. They are found in political organizations, special-interest groups, and individuals with uncompromising opinions on certain topics. These folks can be the nicest, friendliest, most helpful people who would never do anything intentionally to hurt another person, except when their sacred cow is touched or spoken about in a manner that they judge to be negative.

Extreme loyalty to any idea, race, or culture is a breeding pool for SCAHs. Unfortunately, to raise a question about someone from another race, ethnicity, religion, gender, or political party opens the speaker to harsh criticism. The SCAH can always accuse the speaker of being prejudiced against his or her group. The main risk for the person challenging the SCAH is that he or she is likely to be called slanderous names such as racist, anti-Semitic, homophobic, anti-Muslim, sexist, or other derogatory names that fit the stereotype.

After graduating from university and attending seminary, I was part of an internship program in Chicago. As one of twelve seminary students from different parts of the country, our goal was to learn how to be urban clergy. Our training included seminars from various groups and individuals in Chicago. The Windy City was known to be racist at the time, and part of our training was learning how racism exists in cities. Many instructors of our program were African American or Hispanic. In my opinion, not one of the students was racist. We were all young and naïve and had little or no experience of urban (large city) ministry.

At one particular seminar, the presenters were three African American men. A lot of excellent information and dialogue was exchanged. At one point, after a number of questions were asked, one of the instructors said to one of students, "That is just a racist question. You are a racist and don't even know it."

Everyone was shocked, including our own professor and the two other African American presenters. We were young, naïve students asking questions about things we did not fully understand. This did not make us racists. However, by just raising questions, this one man pegged us all as racists. That exchange itself was a learning experience for us all.

My undergraduate, four-year degree (BA) in university was Middle Eastern studies. Afterward I spent four more years studying for a master's of theology that included numerous courses in Old Testament studies as well as anthropology and history courses about the Middle East. After seminary, I became an urban minister of several churches.

One of my weekly responsibilities was to teach Bible classes that included books of the Old Testament, Jewish history, and Middle Eastern history. While not claiming to be an expert in the field, my extensive formal training and weekly studies in the field provided me with information that went beyond the layperson's knowledge and equipped me to teach the subject. I share this to say that I know a little bit about Middle Eastern history, and this informs the background to the next case study.

After buying a condo in a seniors' community in southern Florida, I learned that Italians from New York originally built the community and then added more units later on but could not fill them. To address this financial crossroads, they had to open up the community to other groups in order to fill the recently built units and pay for the new condos.

After several years, the demographic of the community changed, with the largest ethnic group being Jewish, followed by Italians, and then the rest of us. Having studied Jewish history all those years, this was like seventh heaven for me, to be able to listen, learn, and see a more personal side to my Jewish studies. My biggest delight was listening to Jewish husbands tell jokes about their marriages. The jokes just rolled endlessly off their lips as the men reveled in telling them.

It was not long before I discovered a sacred cow in this community. The sacred cow fixation for a very small number of my Jewish friends was Israel. This discovery came out after several general discussions in which Israel came up. Because of my studies of the Middle East, I was able to contribute to discussions on the subject. A problem arose if anything I shared reflected poorly on Israel, either in its past or current history, even though the information was true. Several times one or two accused me of being anti-Semitic for sharing what was the truth.

Even after the issue was immediately fact-checked and my point proved accurate, the accusation of anti-Semitism hotly persisted from a few. In their opinion, the only reason I knew all these things was because I was anti-Semitic and I wanted to criticize Israel.

I responded, "I know these things because I have spent most of my adult life studying and teaching the subject."

This explanation made no dent in their armor defending their sacred cow. These few folks and those like them who condemn, finger-point, and have knee-jerk reactions when their sacred cow is touched are sacred cow assholes (SCAHs).

My father was raised on a farm in Missouri. The last thing he wanted to be was a farmer. He studied, read, and prepared for a career off the farm. He was attending the University of Missouri as World War II broke out. He joined the army and chose his field of service before he was drafted. He enlisted in the army and elected to specialize in artillery because it was far from the front line.

He was in artillery school in Massachusetts, where he met my mother. The Allies were preparing for the D-Day invasion, and my father was yanked out the artillery school and shipped to an infantry unit that landed in France one week after D-Day. He earned two bronze stars for bravery and three purple hearts for being wounded. He returned home after marrying my mother and was determined to have a career.

He finished university with a degree in journalism and photography. He went on to be the editor of fifteen different farm journals in five Midwest states. He fulfilled his dream of not being a farmer and being a successful businessman. He loved his job and won numerous awards for his work. He idolized the business world and all it gave him.

For a few years, our family lived in Cleveland, which was notorious for the Cuyahoga River, which runs through it, catching fire repeatedly. It was known as one of the most polluted rivers in the United States. When we moved to Bay Village on the west side of Cleveland, people were restricted from swimming in Lake Erie because it was so polluted from the Cuyahoga River. In the late 1960s, we lived in this beautiful suburban neighborhood that hosted a wonderful beach. The only problem was that no one could swim in the lake because of the pollution.

My father and I had numerous discussions about the polluted condition of Lake Erie and the Cuyahoga River. He defended the right of companies to pollute the water if it helped their business. After all, these businesses created jobs for residents, and if the jobs were not there, then neither would the residents be there.

I asked how he would feel if the water supply on his farm were polluted and it killed their livestock. He said that would not happen and people should be thankful they had jobs. Fish were dying, people using the water were getting rashes, residents were getting sick, and water sport–related business could not thrive in these conditions. In my father's opinion, cleaning up the river was out of the question if it resulted in companies losing some profit. When a business takes precedent over family, people's health, communities' enjoyment, and the pollution of natural resources, then business has become a sacred cow. My father never budged from his views.

What are the choices in dealing with SCAHs?

1. We must remember that the communication arena is not rational. This is not about facts or reason. It's about deep, extreme, entrenched beliefs that, for the most part, will not be changed.
2. We must realize that the SCAH is a human being just like others and deserves respect and kindness regardless of his or her beliefs; even if his person is offensive and rude in defending his or her sacred cow.
3. The old AA premise, "If a person has breath, there is hope," is applicable.
4. When engaging a SCAH, think through what you want the relationship to be with this person and the consequences you are prepared to live with.

There are numerous responses to dealing with a SCAH, and these choices depend on what kind of a relationship you want with a person, how deeply you feel about the subject, and how much energy you want to expend. This litany of reflections is important because it will determine how one responds, either with a hotly contested challenge, just walking away, or changing the relationship.

One option in dealing with a SCAH is to change the relationship. This does not mean giving up on the other person, disrespecting him or her, or abandoning the individual. It is recognizing that people and situations change. People alter their interest and involvement with others on a regular basis. Throughout all peoples' lives, relationships transform for a variety of reasons, such as a change in vocation, a newly acquired interest or hobby, meeting other people, or just outgrowing the other person.

Whether good or bad, relationships just change. While something may be lost, like time spent together with the other person, other things are gained, like freedom to explore new avenues and meet different people. You can change the relationship without the guilt.

Sometimes it is best to just ignore the comment and try to change the subject. Like any conversation, if one is not invested in the topic or the relationship, or the time is just not right for a heated discussion, then ignore the comment and don't go there. Wait for a better time.

Another alternative is to address the topic. Share your opinions, present facts, fact-check the information, and listen to the other side. If the other person refuses to deal with the topic in a fair and open manner, recognize his or her tactic and deal with it accordingly. Share with the person how you believe they are handling the discussion.

SCAHs use either the pivot or the blame tactic in order to deflect attention away from the faults of their group. For example, if the speaker states a fact that a person from a SCAH's group committed a wrong and the SCAH denies the statement, then fact-check it immediately. Do not let the SCAH pivot off it. Continue to ask the question repeatedly until the SCAH deals with it in an honest manner.

Another tactic used by the SCAH is to bring up an example of someone from another group who committed the crime. They attempt to shift blame to the other person's crime rather than the crime committed by someone from their group. After every pivot attempt, ask, "All right, but what about the wrongdoing that was first mentioned?" "What is your response to that action?" "Is your party responsible for that action, and what should the consequences be?"

The other party may attempt to continually dodge trying to avoid responding to its group's wrongdoing. At this point, the SCAH can be told there is no need to continue the conversation until it can be done in a fair and honest manner. End the dialogue, and try not to get trapped into reopening it until the person can show some honesty and objectivity. Reassure the SCAH that you will continue the dialogue only if it is open and equitable. You have left the door open and have set your terms for involvement.

Another ploy of the SCAH is to blame the speaker or accuse him or her of being racist, homophobic, anti-Semitic, misogynistic, or some other slanderous name in order to divert attention from the topic. This is the SCAH's "Hail Mary pass" when his or her back is against the wall. Even though this person is making it personal, do not take the bait. Again the choice is to confront or ignore to varying degrees. Even if one chooses not to engage fully, it is helpful to not let the slanderous remark go unchecked.

The speaker can simply say, "I am disappointed to hear you make that comment about me because it is certainly not true in any fashion."

The speaker can decide how much and to what degree he or she wants to defend against these slanderous comments. Depending on how desperate the SCAH is, he or she may continue the indictment against the speaker. In this case, the speaker can again state his or her objection and confront or disengage.

At this point, the speaker should seriously consider changing his or her relationship with the SCAH. The reason for this action is that the speaker is worth too much as a person to be treated in this slanderous fashion and should not allow the SCAH to continue the abuse. Besides, it is a terrible waste of time.

Abortion is one of the most fiercely debated topics in America today. This topic draws heated anger from both sides of the aisle and has the potential to alienate folks like no other issue. Unfortunately this is a topic where facts can't be gathered, assimilated, prioritized, or agreed upon to bring the discussion to a rational conclusion. There is a void in our ability to come to a conclusion because of unanswerable questions: When is the fetus a human? Is a fetus a human? What is life? When does human life begin? The interpretations of these questions produce life-and-death consequences in the minds of those involved. This makes the debate over abortion one of our greatest sacred cow issues in America.

The simple pro-life argument is that the fetus is a human fetus, as opposed to a canine fetus, elephant fetus, baboon fetus, or any other mammal fetus. It is a human fetus, and it is living. Therefore it is reasoned that the fetus is a living human. So to terminate the fetus is to terminate something that is human and something that is alive. Termination of a living human is murder.

The other side does not accept this reasoning. The "right to choose" proponents declare that women ought to have the right over their bodies and government (which mainly consists of men) does not have the right to determine what women are or are not allowed to do with their bodies. These sides are at two polar extremes.

Former US republican senator John Danforth from Missouri, also an ordained Episcopal priest and the author of *Faith and Politics*, offers a path of hope. He faced the challenge of dealing with controversial and divisive issues in Congress. Senator Danforth is a committed pro-life antiabortionist who had to meet this challenge in halls of Congress where laws are made that determine how the United States will deal with abortion in America. He naturally argued vigorously in Congress for his pro-life convictions, but he became concerned about how he saw his side dealing with the issue. His most severe criticism was toward the Christian Right.

Danforth claims the greatest weakness of the Christian Right is their certainty about issues. He writes, "Hence the popularity of conservative Christianity with its confidence that it comprehends God's will and can translate it into public policy." If that is their position, how can they back away or compromise the will of God? Danforth maintains that no one knows the will of God because we are not God, and God works in ways that mortals do not always understand. Therefore, our certainty of the will of God and policymaking needs to be tempered with what he calls the Love Commandment, the filter through which our decisions and policymaking should be sifted. He argues this approach for all issues.

His concern over certainty applies not only to people of faith but to all people and all groups. The problem with certainty is that it stifles finding common ground, creativity, and compromise and usually ends with the one who is certain demeaning and finding fault with the other person. This leads to broken relationships, a toxic working environment, divisiveness, discord, blame, and distrust. Trying to reach compromise in this environment is almost impossible. While this situation is difficult, it is not impossible to achieve some degree of benefit for all involved. Three premises of this book are as follows:

1. If there is breath, there is hope.
2. Always leave an open door.
3. Treat others with respect.

Adhering to these three premises creates a positive relationship in which to work and where people have greater chance of listening and hearing one another. Using the listening skills from chapter two, each side can learn what the other side's interests and needs are. From here, a negotiation can begin that explores possible ways of finding common ground. Danforth put forth the concept of the Love Commandment, which calls for everyone to seek to do good for others. The fullness of the Love Commandment is to look for the most that can be done for others and not the least.

In these types of negotiations, both participants should always prepare themselves for the reality that they will not get everything they want. It prevents disappointment and prepares one to consider different possibilities. With open eyes and hearts, ways can be found to help those in need. These two groups can meet and look for ways to do the least harm to those involved instead of trying to get everything one's way.

In order to prepare for this type of dialogue, a helpful exercise is to reframe the situation so as to put one in a more compatible frame of mind. Hence, to invoke the Love Commandment. The following is an exercise I suggest to people who are to be engaged in a high-risk negotiation that could easily lead to judging and blaming others.

Picture a young girl who has been warned repeatedly not to leave her yard and to stay out of the street. The young child knows this since she hears it every time she goes out to play. One day in the heat of play, a ball goes over the fence, out of the yard, and onto the street. She darts out of the yard onto the street to get the ball. A car hits her hard, and she is knocked to the side of the road.

Her parents hear the screech of brakes, the loud thud, and their daughter's scream. What should the parents' response be? Their daughter had clearly disobeyed the rules by leaving the yard and going into the street. The parents have several choices:

1. They can ignore the situation. The little girl disobeyed and got herself into this trouble, so she can get herself out of it.
2. They can go to her, remind her of the rules, and ask her what she has learned from this experience.

Neither of these seem to adhere to the Love Commandment.

3. They can rush to their daughter, call for assistance, embrace her, and tell her that they love her and will do all they can to help her.

The final option is the beginning of the Love Commandment.

When people make mistakes, there are consequences, for example, they experience hurt in some way. A love response is to figure out how to help ease that hurt as well as help correct the mistake. In the case of the young girl who got hit by the car, most normal caring people would look after the girl's injuries and deal with lessons learned later. The same can be said about those who are faced with the decisions on whether to have an abortion. A young girl who becomes pregnant by incest, rape, or curiosity is hurting. The Love Commandment calls for a response to address the girl's hurt and deal with the lessons learned later.

At some point in time, a young girl considering an abortion will, in conjunction with her family, make a decision to have the procedure or not. Those discussions need to be done in a sensitive manner. After exploring all the options, a decision will be made one way or another. How will those who disagree with her decision, whatever it is, treat the young girl? Will it be condemnation or an attempt to be civil, respectful, and understanding? Family, friends, and neighbors are going to impact this child, regardless of their position on abortion. The Love Commandment encourages the treatment of the person first and one's opinion on the matter second.

One never needs to give up his or her beliefs or stop advancing his or her position just because others disagree with him or her. Divisive issues that separate people still require respect for the personhood of others. People can disagree without damaging or demeaning others. Even when deciding, local, state, or federal policies, can be reached that protect the dignity and humanity of all people.

Lessons Learned

1. *Issues that are important to people are important.*
2. *Respect people and the issue.*
3. *Sacred cow arguments are not about reason; nor are they about you.*
4. *Determine the relationship you want with SCAH.*
5. *Relationships are never set in stone.*
6. *Determine what you expect from the relationship.*
7. *Don't get sidetracked from your point.*
8. *Try not to take insults personally. Reason has given way to desperation.*

Guided Responses

1. *Frame responses to maintain respect for the person and his or her issues.*
2. *Leave the situation with an open door to continue the dialogue.*
3. *Set the standard and guidelines for the discussion.*
4. *Keep your values but don't hurt others.*

Activity Sheet

1. **What areas of your life might others say are your sacred cows?**

   ____

   ____

2. **How did you respond the last three times one of these issues was raised?**

   a. ______________________________

   ____

   b. ______________________________

   ____

   c. ______________________________

   ____

3. **Write out three changes you could make using the skills in chapter two to improve responses.**

   a. ______________________________

   ____

   b. ______________________________

   ____

   c. ______________________________

   ____

Ichneumon Wasps

Some creatures enjoy hurting other creatures. Ichneumon wasps may be the cruelest critters on earth. While many creatures need to kill others in order to survive, most of these deaths occur quickly. The Ichneumon wasp pricks its prey and deposits its eggs into the victim. This action paralyzes the prey but keeps it alive. Then the wasp begins to eat its victim alive. It consumes the digestive organs first, which keeps the victim alive and suffering as long as possible. Unfortunately some people are like the Ichneumon wasps. They make others suffer as much as they can. To have a boss with these tendencies is a daily painful grind. Getting away as soon as possible before you are devoured is a clear and reasonable option.

Four

Boss Asshole (BAH)

"Trapped like a rat." This is how many employees feel when working for a boss who is an asshole and makes their lives unpleasant to miserable on a daily basis. Unfortunately your mortgage, career, livelihood, and well-being depend upon your job. There is only one word to describe how employees in this situation should respond.

One of my favorite movies, *The Last of the Mohicans*, directed by Michael Mann, gives an excellent example of this type of situation and how one needs to respond. In the story, the English garrison at Fort William Henry has been defeated by the French and their Native American allies. When promised safe conduct, the English garrison surrender and march out of the fort and begin their journey home.

Along the way, natives ambush them. The hero of the story, Hawkeye, his friend Uncas, and Uncas's father, a Mohican chief named Chingachgook, escape with the two daughters of the English commander, Cora and Alice Munro, and an English officer, Major Duncan.

Fleeing for their lives, they take refuge in a cave under a waterfall. Their reprieve is short because they see their pursuers coming for them. The situation is hopeless. They are now trapped in this cave under a waterfall and are greatly outnumbered.

Hawkeye turns to his flame, Cora Munro, and says, "You, Alice, and Major Duncan are safe because you are valuable to them. They will trade you for money and supplies, but they will kill Chingachgook, Uncas, and me because we are a threat to them. Survive, and I will find you. Survive."

Hawkeye and his two native friends then jump from the cave into the water below. In the end, they do rescue Cora, but the others die.

Survive. This is the message to all those who are trapped working for an asshole company or working for an asshole boss. First and foremost, you need to survive with the least amount of damage to you. There are numerous survival tactics to implement in this type of situation that will be discussed later in this chapter.

Broadly speaking, there are two types of situations in which employees can feel trapped and fearful because their livelihood depends on their employment. The first is working in a situation in which the boss is an outright, unapologetic AH who seems to enjoy making those under him or her miserable. Fortunately most of my working career was as a pastor of a church where I did not have an immediate boss. A church board of deacons oversaw me.

For this type of situation, I will share a military experience that highlights an AH boss. The military is an organization with a clearly defined chain of command, which is rigidly divided into two major groups, officers and enlisted persons, some of whom are noncommissioned officers. There are rules with severe consequences that forbid social interaction between the two groups. To disobey a command from someone who outranks you carries a wide variety of punishments, from being fined, court-martialed, jailed, or executed. In the military, you learn to obey and to follow orders immediately.

The military is unlike civilian organizations. In the military, you can't just quit and go and find another job. You go where they tell you to go. Transfers can be requested, but there is no guarantee. Special assignments and training can be requested, but again there are no guarantees. Talk about being trapped. Here, if you find yourself with an AH boss, you have to find ways to endure. I am very proud of my military service and most of the officers and enlisted persons I served with.

I was *not* an officer in the military, but that of an enlisted person. In other words, my position was from the bottom looking up. Many people outranked me and could exert their authority over me. As stated earlier, there are assholes in every organization on earth. If there are AHs in religious organizations, then it certainly holds true that there are assholes in the military at every level. While it is unpleasant to be around AHs, it is even more unpleasant to be around an AH who has power over you.

Unfortunately some people who have power, whether in civilian or military life, abuse it and enjoy seeing others squirm under their authority. These folks are assholes plain and simple. They don't have to be, but they choose to be. My first encounter with an AH officer came during my basic training at Fort Knox, Kentucky. About twenty of us were loaded on trucks after lunch and taken to a large auditorium, where we were instructed to set chairs out on the main floor of an auditorium. The officer in charge, a second lieutenant, gave us instruction on how the chairs were to be arranged and then left.

We began setting the chairs in place, as he instructed. About four hours later, the lieutenant returned. He walked into the auditorium and began to yell that this was not the way the chairs were to be arranged. All us were privates, so no one was really in charge.

However, I walked over to the officer and said, "I am sorry, sir. We thought this was the way you instructed us to put the chairs."

He responded, "Yes, you are sorry! You are a very sorry individual and a disgrace to the uniform you wear! What the hell were you thinking, private?"

I again said, "I am sorry for this…"

He cut me off and started again about what a sorry individual I was.

Even though we had followed his instructions the first time, he ordered all the rows to be changed and placed in another way. He then left again. We started to redo the chairs and were about 20 percent done when our trucks arrived to take us back for supper.

One of the other privates asked, "What should we do?"

I said, "We have orders to go back and eat, so we get on the trucks and go back and eat."

We left, and that was the last we heard of it. A person in charge can be in charge and accomplish his or her mission without being an asshole and belittling those under him or her.

This seems like a very minor incident in the larger scope of the Vietnam War that was raging at the time. The major consequence of this officer's behavior and those like him is that it breeds contempt and distrust for AH officers. Those negative feelings that I and thousands of others like me developed for officers went with us when we arrived in Vietnam. The consequences of contempt and distrust of this type of officer were much more serious in Vietnam than chairs not being arranged in a certain way.

When under the command of an asshole, people do what is necessary to protect themselves. Leaders of organizations who are assholes do untold damage to others. In the long run, asshole behavior by leaders hurt an organization and the goals they hope to accomplish.

A second situation in which folks feel trapped as employees is when they are in an organization that does not value them or take care of them. In this situation, many employees and management are decent people. However, organizational policies and the way the establishment functions as a whole devalues employees. This damages those in the organization and can sabotage its objectives. This is systemic assholeishness. Unfortunately, many good people are trapped in the clutches of an asshole organization.

My last nine years of employment were with the Broward County Board of Education in Broward County, Florida. My wife and I moved to Florida to help my father, who was caring for my mother, who had Alzheimer's. We quit our teaching jobs in Ontario, Canada, sold our house, some of our furniture, and moved close to my parents so we could care for them.

The Broward School District had promised to transfer our teaching experience and our related teaching experience when we accepted jobs, putting us at a higher pay scale than a teacher coming in at the entry level. To our surprise, we were not given credit for our full experience and began at a very low pay level. I was told that, even though I had teaching experience, very little of it would go to my credit because my prior teaching was not with severely emotionally disturbed students. The board hired me as an Exceptional Student Education (ESE) teacher to teach history.

Since most of my former teaching was not specifically with ESE students, the board did not credit me with those years of teaching experience. To add insult to injury, Broward bragged about being the fourth-largest school district in the nation but did not mention their teacher pay ranked third to the lowest in the whole nation in 2005. This ridiculous low pay does not reflect an organization that values its teachers.

To make matters worse, teachers had a union, but it was emasculated because Florida was and is a work-to-rule state. Functionally that meant teachers could have a union, but they could not strike for fair pay or working conditions. Striking in a work-to-rule state is against the law with penalties of fines and jail time. It is easy to see how the school district could control and abuse teachers with these laws in place.

In spite of the minimal pay and little, if no, representation, my first seven years working for Broward was tolerable because of the staff and administration at my school. Cross Creek School was a center that serviced students from grade one to twelve who were categorized as "severely emotionally disturbed." Later our center was referred to as an emotional behavioral disorders (EBD) center. All the students at Cross Creek were classified as EBD, and most were on at least one medication.

For roughly 120 students, Cross Creek had two nurses, ten therapists, eleven security guards, one deputy sheriff, two behavior specialists, and two ESE specialists. Besides this abundance of staff, our school had three isolation areas and four separate padded isolation rooms. It goes without saying that things got wild some days.

My first seven years working at Cross Creek were rewarding because teachers and staff were valued and we saw our students getting an education and growing in life skills they needed to function in the adult world. In my eighth year, the school district combined two EBD centers. The other center was much newer with more facilities and located in a nicer community. In the wisdom of the school board, they chose Cross Creek to house both schools. Our school was located three hundred yards from one strip club, a half-mile from another strip club, and three-quarters of a mile from a third strip club. There was a McDonald's on the corner.

The closing of the other EBD center led to a huge community fight between the school board and parents concerning the merger, but to no avail. The board ignored them and crammed staff and students into our school. Overcrowding was only one of the problems. Most folks believed this decision was against the students' best interests.

There were all kinds of rumors as to why our principal of sixteen years retired. Rumor had it that the district wanted the other newer school building for their administrative use, and they wanted a fresh start with a new principal. The school was given a new principal, but one who had never been a principal before. Naturally with this kind of arrangement, a great deal of adjustment was needed from all of us.

We buckled our seat belts and prepared for a ride. No one ever imagined what a wild ride it turned out to be. What most of us did not realize in the beginning was the functioning and philosophy of our center was to take a radical change. This change was never presented to us, but it became clear as time went on.

All the team loved and respected our high-school team leader of over sixteen years. Things began to go very badly at the school. About four months into the school year, at a scheduled high-school team meeting, our team leader said, "Things have changed, and I am resigning as team leader."

Everyone was crushed. What had gone so wrong? To mention a few things, eight of our security guards had gone to the hospital for student-related injuries. Some went several times. A student beat one of our female teachers so badly that she was hospitalized and out of school for two weeks. Security could not keep students in isolation rooms, so students took advantage of the situation and roamed freely about the campus, doing whatever they wanted. Finally, teachers were instructed to lock their doors because some of the wanderers entered classrooms and attacked other students.

This was the first time we teachers locked our doors. This action was not to protect us from outsiders, but from our own students. The behavior specialist, a non-teacher with no teaching experience, told students they did not have to obey teacher's instructions and excused student's inappropriate behavior. This gave them license to disobey and behave badly in the classroom and common areas of the school. Fights between students became routine. The new philosophy, which teachers came to learn, was that they, the teachers, were to blame for students' bad behavior.

The new philosophy and change in our school was blurted out in our first high-school meeting of the year. The new behavior specialist, a non-teacher, told us if teachers would teach better, there would be no behavior problems. Several of us asked this person if she knew what kind of school she was in. After a few other insulting remarks, the high-school team leader asked the behavior specialist not to attend our meetings in the future. The principal intervened and ordered the behavior specialist to be allowed in the meetings because we were a team.

The year continued to be a train wreck, going from bad to worse. Numerous letters and complaints had been sent to the school superintendent and school board. Unfortunately, there was no attempt to rescue attempt our train wreck by the school board or the district.

A number of teachers and staff resigned or transferred out because the inmates were now running the asylum. At the end of the year, we thought a new plan was to be put in place that would help the situation. When we returned in the fall, we were introduced to the new strategy, which shockingly was just the opposite of what we had asked for. Now, students who threatened teachers or other students, turned over desks or tables, trashed a room, or refused to comply and were sent out of the class could reenter the classroom in ten minutes. There were no effective consequences as there had been before.

Now a security guard or the behavior specialist, neither of whom had any educational experience, could approve the student's return to class after he or she had threatened, attacked another student, or trashed the classroom. The first week with students, two security guards went to the hospital with student-related injuries, and one student went to the hospital with his head cut open, which required numerous stitches.

The educational component of our school was no different. During the first week of preparation without students, the principal called several meetings with the whole staff to go over housekeeping issues and outline the new procedures for the year. At one of these meetings, the principal talked about the school's approach to teaching classes. She informed staff of our EOC scores—the mandatory state tests given at the end of the year. Staff were informed that my students had scored the highest on the EOC exams in the school and those scores would match any regular high school in the district. There was a round of applause, and I thanked her for the compliment.

The next day I received an e-mail from a curriculum person hired by our school, and he informed me how I was now to teach. To add insult to our teachers, the behavior specialist who had told us the previous year that all student behavioral problems could be corrected if only we teachers would teach better was hired as our new education specialist. This person had never taught in a classroom, bragged about not knowing curriculum, and was now to judge our teaching.

While this was against union policy, administration circumvented it by claiming their observations were just to see if the students were responding to our teaching. We were told it was not an evaluation of our teaching. Naturally everyone saw through this and complained. They should have provided rubber waders for all the bullshit that was being dropped on us.

We were trapped in a school district that did not value its teachers and a school that was either incompetent or very badly misguided. Whether incompetence or misguidance, teachers and staff were getting hurt physically, emotionally, and spiritually. Students were also losing out at the best education they could have gotten and learning helpful life skills.

So what do you do in a situation like this? My response was a multilevel approach. First, I talked with other teachers to understand their perceptions. Next, I talked with my team leader. And from there, our team had numerous discussions about the decline in our school. The team leader, on our behalf, met repeatedly with the principal to discuss our concerns. Other teachers and I spoke individually with the principal to share our concerns. The principal, in turn, addressed our concerns in staff meetings.

The message from these meetings was clear. We were to fall in line and comply with the new directions. As things continued to get worse, several teachers and staff wrote letters to the district and school board, explaining our situation. For my part, I wrote two letters to our district administrator, but I did not even get the courtesy of a response. I wrote a formal complaint of a student who threatened to kill me repeatedly and who would run up and yell in my ear from behind, causing me pain.

My complaint, which was to be addressed and investigated in one week according to district policy, took two months. When I met with a district representative concerning this situation, he asked, "What do you expect us to do? We can't do anything. What are your suggestions?"

I informed him I was a teacher, but then I gave him some suggestions that had worked in the past. These he dismissed. I sent a letter to the superintendent and received no response.

By the end of the school year, our school was in disarray, certainly from a teacher's perspective. However, at the very end of the year, a thin ray of light promised some hope. We came back for the new school year with the prospect that things were going to be better. As stated earlier, the first week with students went horribly awry. The light at the end of tunnel had been extinguished.

In light of this, I weighed my options. I had wanted to continue and retire with two friends at the end of this new school year. For my physical and mental health, I retired immediately. This was possible for me because my Social Security and Medicare were in place, and I knew I could secure a part-time job. I felt like Hawkeye jumping out of the cave into the water and away from danger. I knew I would never return and my friends would remain on their own. This was painful.

When I left, the prominent feeling I experienced was guilt, that is, guilt in leaving behind some dear people who had to stay in a desperate situation. After retiring, I made one last effort to help my colleagues by making a presentation before the school board with the superintendent present. They smiled and thanked me for coming, but nothing was ever said to me after my presentation. My former colleagues at school told me no one ever came to investigate and things continued to get worse. This was a lose-lose situation, especially for the students.

What can you do when you are trapped working for an asshole boss or in an asshole organization? You can consider the following:

- Survive.
- Keep cool, and take it slow.
- Remember that it is *not* about you. It is about the AH boss or AH organization.
- Recall that the old boxing adage says, "Protect yourself at all times." Write everything down.
- Think long term, and be strategic.
- Seek advice from trusted friends and colleagues.
- Establish a trusted in-house support group.
- Write out your options, and evaluate them with friends.
- Do an honest search for what you really want out of life and what it will take to get there.
- Set your eyes on your goal.
- Do the best work you can do under the circumstances.
- If you leave, do so with a plan and a backup in place.
- Do the best for yourself, and have no regrets.

Activity Sheet

If you make the decision to leave your place of employment, do it in a way that benefits you and does not hurt you.

1. Take your time and work smartly through your actions.
2. Think anew about the type of work you want to do, and *make a list* of those jobs.
3. Write out a strategy with time schedules to direct and implement your move.
4. Use an employment company to advise you, help you prepare for the move, research possibilities that match your skills, and locate available positions.

5. Use the internet to research companies, prepare for interviews, write a résumé, and do job searches.
6. Write out a short and clear statement as to why you are leaving and what you are looking for. Be short on the negative and long on the positive.
7. Write out a list of your skills and what contribution you bring to a company.

Naked Mole Rat

Many consider this rodent to be one of the ugliest creatures on earth. The mole rat is a hairless rodent with two big beaver-like teeth. Even their mothers have a hard time looking at their young. Of course, these rats live mainly underground and are almost blind, so attractiveness is not a high priority. One queen rules the colony, and she kills any female that challenges her and severely abuses the other females by biting and kicking them out of resting areas. While only three or so males impregnate the queen, the rest of the rats are workers, food gatherers, or protectors of the colony. Besides being ugly, they have a disgusting habit of eating their feces for added nourishment. Over time, humans have gravitated toward political forms of government that are participatory and not trial by combat. We choose our leaders and set moral standards to guide our behavior. Our form of government has checks and balances so no one person or group can get too powerful and abuse others.

Five

Bigoted Asshole (BAH)

I have held a belief for a long time that everyone is prejudiced toward others in some form or another. Certainly there are folks who will challenge this assertion; however, I believe that an honest examination will reveal that all people are a little prejudiced toward some group. No matter how well intended a person is and regardless how hard he or she works at being open, loving, and nonjudgmental, prejudice toward a group he or she is unfamiliar with will eventually seep out. The good news is that this does not make people AHs. Mostly these folks are wonderful, kind individuals who work hard at not being prejudiced and deserve respect and praise for their effort and good intentions.

However, if that tiny bit of prejudice is left unchecked, it can easily evolve into bigotry and hate. When this happens, the person becomes a bigoted asshole (BAH). There are thousands of different types of people on whom bigots can spew out their disgust and contempt. In the United States, every race on earth is represented. Unfortunately scientists can't agree on the criteria for what constitutes race or even how many races there are on earth. The debate is somewhere between zero and eight. Believe it or not, there are those who argue with evidence that race does not even exist.

If race is not enough to find differences between people, then ethnicity greatly expands that spectrum. Scientists are again uncertain about how to define or count ethnicity. Some scientists claim there are as many as 141 different ethnic groups in the world, not counting the different number of tribes on each continent. If these are included, the number more than doubles, and if the subgroups of all the ethnic classes and tribes are counted, the differences are astronomical. Almost all of these ethic groups and their subgroups are found in the United States, and they speak over 380 different languages and dialects. Depending on how diversity is calculated, the United States ranks number one in the world by some counts according to population and as low as eighty-fifth using other criteria.

In short, the United States has thousands of differences between people based on race, language, ethnicity, regionalism, culture, heritage, and religion. The United States is further divided by geography, climate, education, wealth, employment, management and unions, political parties, the cities, suburbs, and the rural areas, to mention a few. Differences often give rise to prejudice, which usually exacerbates to hatred, which grows like an uncontrollable fungus.

The most obvious division among people is gender. The United States is almost evenly divided, with 51 percent women and 49 percent men. There has always existed a love-hate relationship between the genders and a great deal of bigotry by a small percentage of men toward women. At first, this disdain for women seems strange because females have always been in a more vulnerable position than men are. This, in part, is due to the fact that most women are smaller and physically weaker than men are. Our evolution as people favored physical strength.

Besides the physical component, women bear children and are most likely to stay with the adolescents, care for the young ones, sacrifice for the kids, and try to protect their offspring. While many men appreciate the women's position and try to help a little, others see this as an opportunity to take advantage of a weaker, more vulnerable person. From this attitude grows an unhealthy and dangerous prejudice and bigotry toward women from some men around the world. This prejudice and bigotry crosses all national boundaries, racial types, and ethnic and cultural groups.

I love the outdoors, and after retiring from teaching, I wanted a job that was outside and on a golf course. A position came up as starter/ranger/cart person on a golf course near my home. It was a total change from teaching, and I loved being outside and close to golf.

One morning my assignment was the starter, which entailed getting prearranged foursomes off at their scheduled times. When players don't have a foursome, they are paired up to others, whom they don't know, in order to make a foursome. The golf shop had scheduled a husband and wife from Quebec, Canada, and two local men to make a foursome and play together. This is standard procedure at any golf course.

On the first tee, one of the two men asked if there were another pairing they could be placed with instead of the couple from Quebec. I knew that some of our locals have a problem with Canadians, especially French Canadians. I informed him the next open spot was in about an hour and a half.

The man frowned and said, "Oh, all right."

They teed off, and that was the end of it. Or so I thought. My fellow worker, the ranger, the person who drives around the course and makes sure no group is playing too slow or having problems, drove up and asked if I would trade places with him for an hour. I agreed.

On my rounds checking the course, the only space between the foursomes came when I saw the French Canadian couple playing by themselves. I could not see the other two men, and the hole behind them had no one on it. I stopped and inquired about the other two gentlemen who had been with them. They informed me the men told them to go on ahead by themselves and they would play behind them as a twosome.

On my way back to see the two men who separated from the Quebec couple, I discovered they were a hole and a half behind the French couple. As I pulled up beside the two men, the man who had asked not to be paired with the French couple yelled out before I could say anything, "I am not going to play with any damn bitch."

Well, that explained a number of things about his original request and his being an asshole. Technically, he could have been instructed to play with the couple or leave the course.

Instead, to avoid an unnecessary conflict, I said, "I am not asking you to play with the couple. Just try to keep up with them. You have fallen a hole and a half behind, so please try to keep up with them so play can move along."

For any golfer, especially a proud, arrogant male, this is an outright insult. To be told you are slower than others are and, in this case, a woman is not something one brags about. His golf partner hung his head, bit his lip, and did not say a word. I drove off to the next hole with a hidden smile on my face and a pleasant thought. *There, take that home, you asshole.*

To further demonstrate the point that men show prejudice against women, the golf course provides another excellent example. Male golfers swear at their golf balls repeatedly when they make a bad shot. This seems rather foolish because the ball went exactly where the golfer hit it. In other words, it is not the ball's fault. When some male golfers miss a shot, they refer to their golf ball as "that bitch." Even the nicest, cleanest, most respected golfers who do not tell dirty jokes or make lewd comments about women will occasionally say, "Damn. That bitch [his golf ball] missed the hole."

Unfortunately some male golfers take this approach to their golf ball to a whole other level. They call their golf balls every nasty female name or part of the body they can imagine. It is so bad at times that other players have to ask the foulmouthed person to clean up his act. Unfortunately, many times, the comments are left unchecked.

During the election, the Republican presidential candidate reopened the topic of misogyny in a colorful, vulgar manner. He smiled and bragged about going into teenage girls' dressing rooms while they were unclothed, grabbing women wherever he wanted, insulting women by calling them names, and focusing on women's body parts. Many, including his wife, excused these actions as boyish behavior and described the verbal references about women as being "locker room talk."

This public display of verbal attacks and insults about women exposed the way some men think about women, the privileged position men have over women, and how a large section of the population, both male and female, accepts this attitude.

When the Republican nominee braggingly claimed he could grab women by their private parts, this led to a national dialogue on sexism. One of my friends, who is very respectful of women and goes out his way to be courteous and kind to women, shared his thoughts and beliefs about the incident. To put his argument into perspective, he is usually most critical of the Republican candidate. My friend argued, though, when guys get together, they talk about women in sexual ways that are just fun and not harmful. He claimed this was true on the block of his old neighborhood as a kid when he was involved in sports and also at his place of business. Men just talk about women that way, but they don't mean anything by it because it is among friends and coworkers and not in front of the ladies.

This, he argued, does not make men misogynists or sexists. It is just the way men are when they are with their friends. His reasoning was supported by others and represents, I believe, the opinion and beliefs of many men in our society. No harm, no foul. Men can say these things, but they are not really sexists if they just say them to one another, not to women, and they don't intend any harm.

My friend is Jewish, so I put his argument to him in Jewish terms.

I asked, "What if people were making stereotypical derogatory remarks about Jewish people, but they were doing it with just their friends and not in front of Jews? Would they then not be anti-Semitic?"

There was a long pause because my friend had been in a few very heated exchanges with a couple of Gentiles who made derogatory remarks about Jews, which came to his attention, and he exploded with accusations of anti-Semitism. In his mind, men making derogatory remarks about women was acceptable, but Gentiles making derogatory statements about Jews was not. There was no meeting of the minds on this issue.

However, the exchange was helpful, for it made my friend think a little. The reason to speak out against this type of language is the hope that those making these kinds of remarks will think twice before saying them again. Who knows? They may have an epiphany and change.

Are people who make derogatory comments about any other group other than themselves assholes? By my definition and construction of AHs, yes, they are. Though they may not mean any harm or ill will to a female or any other group, they continue to contribute to a sexist, racist culture. By my definition, they are a special type of AH. They are bigoted AHs (BAHs). Some might argue that they mean no ill intent when putting down the other gender, races, ethnic groups, religions, or classes of people. However, I contend a put-down is a put-down. Disrespecting another person or group hurts, whether it is intentional or not. In the larger scope of community, it hurts the whole community because it breeds contempt, mistrust, and negativity.

There are different ways to deal with BAHs. First, there is the truly obnoxious, hurtful, unapologetic bigot. In this case, the woman hater who would not play a round of golf with a woman is an unreasonable and unchangeable person who is most likely not going to alter his attitude or behavior toward women. It is not known what brought on his hatred, but it is inexcusable to brand and abuse all women for something that might have happened to him in the past by a woman. In cases like this, we do not usually have the time to try to untangle his twistedness. If time and opportunity persists, one can always try, but the current situation still needs to be addressed in real time.

The French couple made a decision not to try to reason with the man or discover why he didn't want to play with them. They did not let him ruin their day, and they just continued to finish their round of golf and enjoy their time together. In like manner, I made the same decision not to confront him or his behavior or challenge his rude remarks. I took the opportunity to deflect his ill-mannered reaction, and in a subtle way, I let him know that his behavior was unacceptable. Another choice would have been to calmly say this is not an appropriate way to talk about women. This is a personal choice based on a number of factors.

This same approach can be taken in like situations. Once when I was at the VA hospital for treatment, an Asian doctor approached another veteran to treat him. Like me, he was also a Vietnam veteran, and he refused for an Asian physician to see him and demanded for a white doctor to treat him. His demands were respectfully granted, and he waited for over three hours so the next available white doctor could see him. Sometimes it is good to let the bigots have their way and let them live with the consequences.

The situation is certainly different in the case of law enforcement. For example, a female or minority police officer who encounters an unresponsive, uncooperative, abusive, and potentially dangerous bigot may need to apply force to protect himself or herself and the public. There are times when the bigot can be accommodated for the good of the community, and there are other moments when the bigot needs to be confronted and made answerable for his or her actions immediately.

In social situations, people encounter BAHs and their bigoted comments and behaviors. These insults and actions can come at any time and in any situation. One disarming yet confrontational response is to let the offending person know that the comment is not welcomed and you hope it will not be stated again. To deliver this message in the most helpful way for the person to hear it and not react negatively is to convey the statement in a nonthreatening manner. This includes tone, facial gestures, and nonaggressive posture. If others join in that request, it reinforces the positive message to change the language and behavior of the BAH.

If this does not alter the situation, it may be time to leave, confront with a stronger language, or call for a person in a position of authority, such as a store manager or the proprietor to intercede. If the situation does not get resolved, then a quick check of possible consequences is in order. If the decision to stay and confront is made, the consequences may be nasty. It is an individual choice.

Learned Lessons

1. *Inform the person that his or her comments are offensive.*
2. *Let him or her know your expectation for appropriate behavior in this setting.*
3. *Seek others' opinions to reinforce the message of inappropriate comments.*
4. *Leave if the situation is unchanged.*
5. *Involve a person in authority to deal with the offensive person.*
6. *Smile and ignore the person.*
7. *Stay and confront the individual, remaining mindful of the consequences.*

Guided Responses

1. *Own your prejudices.*
2. *If in doubt, ask friends or associates in what ways they may see you as prejudiced.*
3. *Ask those folks what specific comments or actions you make that demonstrates prejudice in their opinion.*
4. *Make an effort to change.*

Activity Sheet

1. **List what you believe are your prejudices. Include those your friends and acquaintances say are yours.**

Race	Ethnic groups	Religion	Nations	Gender	Sexual Orientation	Other *Poor, Rich, Uneducated, and so on.*

2. **Write out specific words or actions that suggest you are prejudiced in these areas.**

____

____

3. **Circle the choice(s) where you think your prejudices originated: family, friends, neighborhood, religion, school, or society.**

4. **Have you met anyone in a group mentioned in question number one that did not fit the stereotype? Yes No**

5. **Write out three ways to show respect for those who are different from you. Use words such as "like," "appreciate," "respect," "understand," "admire," and "commend," to mention a few.**

   a. ____

   ____

   b. ____

   ____

   c. ____

   ____

Praying Mantis

When some creatures get in certain situations, their innate behavior takes over, and it can get quite bizarre. The female praying mantis, for whatever reason, eats the head off the male during mating. At least she doesn't have to worry about him running off and being with another female. When excitement or anger floods humans, they can learn to control their emotions and minimize damage to others. We can exert ourselves and say, "Stop! I don't like that!" We can also learn that no means no and stop.

Six

Events Asshole (EAH)

EAHs are normal people because they act in socially acceptable ways in most situations. They can be fun, interesting, and appropriate folks most of the time. They usually contribute in a positive fashion and are not the type of people who will embarrass others or themselves. However, there is the odd time when they are at a special event and become transformed into "bizarro" people, or EAHs, as they will be referred to here. This is the out-of-control hockey mom who trains her kids to mind their manners at home and then goes berserk at the hockey game if she thinks the referee has made a bad call against her son. She yells at the referees, screams at other players, hollers at other fans, bangs on the glass, pounds on the seats, rips up programs, makes obscene gestures, and squawks like a seagull throughout the game.

In other environments, she is a very nice, pleasant, caring person. However, at this single event, she is an asshole, plain and simple. It is nice to see someone free and expressive. Nevertheless, once that enthusiasm turns to uncontrollable outbursts and gyrations that demean others, it is unpleasant and abusive to all.

Unfortunately EAHs are not limited to just sports fans. They can be at any type of event where there is a crowd of passionate people such as a rock concert, political rally, school board or town-hall meeting, theater, art show,

Christmas party, workshops, religious gatherings, holiday events, plays, or the opera. Yes, even the opera can be an excellent place to observe EAHs at their best. This is such an extreme opposite of the beer guzzling, foulmouthed hockey mom. While the behavior appears totally different, the painstaking suffering of listening to a rabid opera enthusiast is just as revolting and abusive as listening to an obnoxious hockey mom.

The opera is a sophisticated, formal, and refined experience. Attenders sit in very comfortable seats, respectful of those around them, and whisper quietly while waiting for the lights to go down and the performance to begin. Once the opera starts, the audience is quietly attentive to the beauty of the music that fills the auditorium.

This type of serenity is to be admired in a day of a thousand distractions and interruptions. Intoxicating sounds carry off the opera listener to a state of melodic and euphoric ecstasy. The atmosphere is as reverent as a house of worship. Operagoers, for the most part, follow a ritual etiquette that seeks to protect the sanctity of the experience. The hallowed hall, almost by osmosis, gently drifts quietly toward the rising of the curtain. Polite and respectful applause is presented to the cast, and the opera begins. All emotions and responses are held until the appropriate time when the audience may clap and express a bravo or two.

When the curtain drops for intermission, those in need quietly shuffle to the washrooms as others meander to the lounge for refreshments and conversation. There is something about curtain dropping that stirs up the assholeishness in a few operagoers. The performance was good and perhaps even exceptional, and this naturally deserves time for praise and an opportunity to relive the moment. Like the hockey mom, there are always those who go bizarro.

These are the operagoers who can't shut up. It is as if they picture themselves as opera stars and the lounge has become their stage. They bellow out note after note of their sanctimonious, grandiose vehemence about the performance that eclipses any exaltations given by religious worshippers to their God.

They are like the hockey mom because they both see only their myopic world that includes no one else. They are shut off from the feelings and thoughts of others. They care only about what is of interest to them at this moment, much like a drug addict. The consensus response from those around the EAH is a silent chorus of, "Please, just shut up and let us enjoy the performance in a reasonable way."

Out of politeness, others listening can either drift off to another part of the lounge or try to change the subject if the speaker takes a breath. These are two responses that listeners can use to defend themselves against an EAH.

Of course there are other options, but for this section, only two will be discussed. One is to tell the person straight out that his or her praise sounds braggadocios. More subtle examples are as follows:

1. "Well, that is certainly an extreme compliment."
2. "My, that is very expressive. Have you thought of being a professional critic?"
3. "I certainly enjoyed the performance but would not rate it quite that high."
4. "How did you come up with all those delicious sounding expressions?"

Another confrontational way to approach the braggart is to say something like, "Yes, we all know it was a great performance, but I think your description exceeds the performance." The weakness of this approach is that it begs the offender to defend himself or herself, which gives this person license to keep talking. This, in turn, defeats the purpose of silencing the critic.

Another technique is to ask others in the group their opinion in order to give them an opportunity to share and silence the EAH. Call on another listener by name and ask him or her what he or she thought. Do this two or three times and intermission is over and you can go back to the sanctity of the auditorium.

However, If the objective is to have a good time and there is nothing else to do at the moment, some might choose to have fun and play the game. This is easily done by using active listening skills. The EAH says, "That was the most extraordinary, divine, rapturous overture I have ever heard."

Play his game by asking, "Really, you think that was the best overture you have ever heard?" Then stand back, enjoy your drink, and watch him perform.

If the EAH spouts off and says, "That aria definitely deserved many bravos tonight," the listener could ask, "It was good. Why do you think it deserved the extended applause?"

Again, this is a time to embrace the moment and listen to the EAH in order to further entertain the group. If you adopt this technique, try not to smile.

Lessons Learned

1. *An EAH can spoil any function.*
2. *A person does not have to be obnoxious to spoil an event.*
3. *Communication skills can be implemented to save the event.*
4. *Others can be enlisted to help with the EAH.*

Guided Responses

1. *Be proactive and mentally prepare for this behavior at these events.*
2. *Think about appropriate responses before the event.*
3. *When the EAH begins, ask those around you what they think of the behavior.*
4. *Confront the behavior involving the support of others.*
5. *Politely ask the offender to desist.*
6. *Gently use sarcasm to help the EAH see his or her offensive actions.*
7. *If necessary, speak with force to the individual.*
8. *If bearable, see it as entertainment.*

Activity Sheet

1. In what situations do you display excitement and anger?

____

____

2. **At what events, do you see people displaying EAH behaviors?**

3. **What is your typical response to these folks in those situations?**

4. **How would you like to respond?**

5. **Write out three different ways you could respond that could help the situation.**
   a. ______________________________
   b. ______________________________
   c. ______________________________

Bedbugs

Bedbugs' normal behavior is to locate a warm spot and settle in for the night. Since they are parasites, they feast on sleeping people. During their feasting, they cause bite marks and rashes on their victims. Like all creatures, they have instant reflexes that are uncontrolled. Even though the female has a reproductive tract, the impatient male will spear his partner in the abdomen to inseminate her. Like the old adage goes, "Where there is a will, there is a way." Humans have developed a protocol that guides our responses in different situations and the capacity to talk through different circumstances. We don't just force the other person to do what we want.

Seven

Knee-Jerk Asshole (KJAH)

Everyone has a bad day. Anyone can make a mistake. It is natural. At times, there might be a specific reason for a bad day, but generally bad days come and go like the wind. I love golf and play six times a week. Golfers say they lose their swing or just can't hit the ball in the sweet spot some days. Yesterday they could have hit it perfectly and had a good score. Today the swing is just off. It is a true mystery. Professional golfers hit between one hundred to one thousand practice balls a day. V. J. Singh is reported to hit one thousand to twelve hundred balls a day. Tiger Woods used to hit almost a thousand balls a day. Other pro golfers hit much less, but they practice all the time to stay on top of their game.

With endorsements, the top golfers make anywhere from $20 million to $100 million a year. In one year, Tiger Woods, at his height, made $15 million playing golf and another $85 million in endorsements. Arnold Palmer, who recently died and hadn't played for ages, still made $40 million just through endorsements. Jordan Spieth made $53 million in 2015, while Rory McIlroy made $48 million.

When these top players go to a major tournament, they have their coaches on site to observe their swing and play. Why? As good as they are and as much as they practice, they make mistakes and want someone there to help correct the errors. Big money is at stake.

If these pros make mistakes, think of the average golfer and the number of mishits he or she makes during a round of golf. Making mistakes and having a bad day happens all the time to everyone. The trick is not to beat yourself up over it, but to correct the mishap as soon as possible and go on.

Unexpected things happen, and people are forced to respond to an incident in the moment. The communication skills mentioned in chapter two can help. Usually there is no time to think, and many of the immediate responses turn out to be knee-jerk reactions. Most folks do not have a million-dollar coach who travels with them to inform them they are making a mistake and then provide instruction on how to correct it. The average golfer knows when he or she hits a bad shot. And usually he or she has an idea of what went wrong, so he or she can self-correct. Besides his or her own knowledge and experience, golf buddies can offer suggestions and advice. The point is that, even though mistakes are made, the average person can work them through with positive results.

When alone, with no one around, knee-jerk reactions may not have serious consequences. For example, if driver A pulls out in front of driver B without looking and almost causes an accident, this can elicit a knee-jerk reaction. Driver B can yell out an obscenity in the confines of his car, which the other driver can't hear, flash a vulgar hand gesture, or rant about how stupid the other driver is. These types of hot outbursts have little effect on the situation, other than to provide the offended driver with an immediate opportunity to vent his or her frustration. Everybody gets home safe.

In the presence of others, knee-jerk reactions can have serious consequences. Even though neither party set out to be an AH, both individuals can end up being AHs. The one can be an unintended action, while the other becomes an AH by his or her response.

Two youths accidentally bump into each other. One, having a bad day or a nasty disposition, snaps back, "Watch out, punk." This could escalate to a physical altercation with the next exchange of words.

Two couples who have been friends for years meet for a dinner date. The husband of one of the couples, Paul, invested in a stock deal that turned sour and cost him a lot of money.

His friend Jerry says, "Well, that wasn't a very good move you made losing all that money."

Paul, who is also having difficulties at work through no fault of his own, feels vulnerable, threatened, and humiliated and fires back, "Thanks for the support. You're not doing all that well either."

In another case, an impatient boss with low self-esteem misses a scheduled appointment. He vigorously stomps up to the administrative assistant's desk and demands, in a demeaning tone, a report that is not due until next week.

The assistant, who was up all night with a sick child, is sleep-deprived and anxious about her daughter. And she is carrying some unresolved conflict about her boss. She fires back in a forceful, undignified tone, "Just be patient and wait. You know it is not due until next week."

Oops, to all three situations.

When in the presence of others, these three cases represent the bulk of when knee-jerk responses occur. The first situation is a casual encounter between strangers, the second involves a relationship between friends, and the third is in the workplace environment.

An excellent book that explores work environment relationships is *The No Asshole Rule* by Robert Sutton. The question again arises about how to deal with these three very different situations.

The knee-jerk asshole (KJAH) is the offending party, but one of the tasks of the responder is to ignore or respond in helpful manner rather than drop down to the AH level and join the offender by retaliating like an AH. In these slippery situations, the ice on the lake is thin, and it would be easy to break through and fall in. While it might feel gratifying for an instant to retaliate, the consequences in all three situations could be unfortunate or unpleasant and have short- or long-term negative consequences.

In the first case, two strangers have an accidental encounter, and one fires off an unpleasant or threatening comment. Generally an apology as a first response resolves the encounter. "Hey, I am sorry. I did not see you."

Some KJAHs have to have the last word and may fire back another insult like, "Yea, well just watch yourself next time." Taking into account consequences, a second response would be to smile, repeat the apology, and then walk away. I have a friend who uses the following technique to disarm an insulting protagonist, "Oh, wow. Are you having a bad day too? I am, and it is just a bummer."

More times than not, the offending person shares his or her own bad day, conflict is avoided, and both parties walk away winners. If the decision is to stay and confront, remember to think through consequences. A confrontational approach normally results in a lose-lose situation. Sometimes wisdom is the better part of valor.

In the second situation, one friend feels insulted and humiliated by another. An excellent approach in a situation among friends is to tell the friend how you feel about his comment. The "I message" described in chapter two is an excellent technique to communicate this message. It goes something like this, "Mike, when you said my investment wasn't very good and I lost a lot of money, it humiliated me and made me want to defend myself or really strike back at you. And that does not make for a pleasant dinner outing."

Another option is to just ignore the comment. This choice could result in harboring resentment, which always has a way of escaping at the wrong time. If there were unusual circumstances that affected the investment, these could be explained to support and defend the original venture.

Another alternative is to redirect the comment away from the offensive statement. A redirected response sounds like this, "In the last several months, investments across the country have declined. The analysts blame foreign substitutes." This takes the investor off the hook and channels the conversation to another course.

The third case takes place in a work environment and demands greater attentiveness to consequences. Folks' jobs and livelihood are at stake, so the response should be approached with the greatest care. In the workplace, active listening skills can give breathing room to collect one's thoughts and responses. Active listening involves stating back to the person (in this case, the boss) his or her initial request. This technique requires the boss to speak again, which provides additional time for the employee to collect himself or herself. An added benefit to this tactic is that it demonstrates to the boss that the employee is listening and asking for further direction. All bosses enjoy being looked to for advice and direction. It is a rarity that the boss will come back and ask, "Didn't you hear me?" The majority of the time, the person will pause and repeat his or her request or make an adjustment to it. This provides needed time to settle and gather responses. When using an active listening technique, use all the avenues available to you. In this case, the assistant can use her unfortunate situation to her advantage.

A helpful response could sound like this, "I am sorry. I have been up all night with my sick child. Did you want the report that is due next week now, or could it wait until next week?" This approach informs the boss of the employee's miserable night and the ill condition of the child. This gives the boss an opportunity to cool off and rethink his or her request and tone.

Another approach is to be proactive. Have a sign on the desk that is *only* used in rare instances. The sign says in bold letters, "**Bad day. Please be patient.**" Another option is to nod affirmatively at the boss, wait a reasonable period, and then approach the boss with an "I message" or explain to him or her why it would be better to wait for the report next week. The secretary could share that, if the report is gathered now, it will be incomplete and other work that is needed today would have to wait. This allows the boss an opportunity to cool off and rethink his or her request.

KJAHs will always be around to pull people's chains. Sadly, this is a fact of life, but the chains do not have to restrict or defeat you. It is regrettable if the offended person gets sucked into retaliating and making the situation worse. Active listening skills and other communication aptitudes are the first line of defense and offense. If used properly, they can deflect an insult, provide time to compose, and offer an appropriate response.

Lessons Learned

1. *Do not interpret the encounter as personal. Most of the time, it is not about you.*
2. *Try to determine what the concern is from the other person.*
3. *Explain your intentions were not meant to offend.*
4. *Accept apology if one is given.*
5. *Look for ways or an opportunity to clear the air.*
6. *Explain your concern.*
7. *Use skills to deal with situation.*

Guided Responses

1. *When encountered with a knee-jerk moment, take a deep breath.*
2. *Own your actions and apologize just for your actions.*
3. *Mentally prepare for these types of situation and have a prepared response.*

Activity Sheet

1. What is your normal reaction in a knee-jerk situation?

____

____

2. List three different situations where an exchange with a KJAH went bad.

a. ______________________________

____

b. ______________________________

____

c. ______________________________

____

3. List changes in your response that could have altered the exchange for the better.

____

____

____

4. **What were the concerns of the other persons in question two?**

   a. ______________________________

   b. ______________________________

   c. ______________________________

5. **Write out a statement for a, b, and c in question four that shows the other party you understand his or her concern.**

   a. ______________________________

   ____

   b. ______________________________

   ____

   c. ______________________________

   ____

6. **Write out a prepared response for a future encounter with a KJAH.**

   ____

   ____

   ____

Chimpanzee

Scientists claim that the chimpanzee's DNA is closer to humans than any other animal. Chimps developed the use of tools that assist them in obtaining food. They take sticks to poke in ant holes to gather ants, they make spears by chewing off the end to make it sharp to spear fish, and they use rocks to crack open nuts. Besides using stones to crack things open, they have been observed throwing rocks to ward off other animals. Things were going well until they started throwing rocks at each other and poking one another with pointed sticks. Their new toys were useful but became hazardous when used inappropriately. We can learn from the animals. Tools can be helpful if used as tools, but not if they become an obsession; they are a distraction from our goals and responsibilities, or they hurt others.

Eight

Tech Asshole (TAH)

Cell phones, smartphones, GPSs, laptops, tablets, e-readers, and the like have become a necessary part of life for those in the modern world. While useful, these devices have a very dark side. Not only are they addictive, they are now a dangerous menace to society. Cell phones and other electronic devices have become a cesspool for asshole behavior. Hence, a new category of AH has been created, the Tech AH (TAH). The leading cause of death among teenagers today is car accidents, and the number-one factor in car accidents among teens is cell-phone use, not alcohol or drugs. That is right. Texting and talking on the cell phone is the leading cause of death among teenagers today. The misuse of these tech devices is pervasive and has not only become harmful in causing unnecessary deaths but also become destructive to developing relationships, parenting, creating new hobbies, or initiating new opportunities. Our tech devices are used to babysit our children, introduce them to extreme violence at a young age, deprive them of socialization skills, cheat them out of human interaction, and instill in them an addiction to these instruments. Jane Brody writes in the *New York Times*, July 6, 2015:

> In its 2013 policy statement on "Children, Adolescents, and the Media," the American Academy of Pediatrics cited these shocking

> statistics from a Kaiser Family Foundation study in 2010: "The average 8 to 10-year-old spends nearly eight hours a day with a variety of different media, and older children and teenagers spend more than 11 hours per day. Television, long a popular 'babysitter,' remains the dominant medium, but computers, tablets and cellphones are gradually taking over."

Believe it or not, parking lots, whether in the suburbs or urban areas, have become one of most dangerous areas in America. One in five vehicular accidents occurs in parking lots. Pedestrian fatalities in parking lots are up 13 percent since 2010. One in four children killed in car accidents occur in parking lots. Why? Cell-phone use is one of the major causes. People get out of their cars, put their phone to their ear, and walk along, oblivious to everything around them. This asshole behavior is just as much a distraction as driving under the influence.

American society is developing an elitist privileged culture that includes the poor. People with cell phones think they can use their cell phones anywhere. Pedestrians step out in the street without looking, thinking and believing that cars should stop for them. They forget the laws of physics that determine how fast a car can stop at any given speed. They embrace their phone like a lover from whom they have been separated for a long period of time. Pedestrians caress their phone, speak passionately to it, and are so wrapped in its embrace that they ignore a two thousand-pound object bearing down on them. The old adage is true. They never knew what hit them.

Being in a car is just as dangerous. While driving on the turnpike at seventy-five miles an hour, cars pass me on the left, and some drivers are talking or texting on their phones. The Department of Motor Vehicles says it takes less than three seconds to get distracted and swerve into another car. At that speed, there is property damage and possibly bodily injury or death. One wonders, "Was the call or text really important enough to endanger lives?" Certainly not, and the National Safety Council informs us that 660,000 assholes make that choice to text and drive, which results in thousands of unnecessary accidents every year.

This obliviousness to surroundings and other people that cell-phone users display has propagated an environment where nothing is sacred. The dividing line between public and private is being erased. Cell phones ring in theaters, plays, doctors' offices, courtrooms, places of worship, and schools. It has become the norm for someone to sit next to a stranger and have a discussion on his or her cell phone. Most of the time, it is not an emergency, but just two buddies having a talk at someone else's expense. For whatever reason, when people are on cell phones, their voices seem to raise more than normal. They don't realize that the person on the other end can hear them just fine, but it is really obnoxious to those sitting around them.

My wife was going to visit her sister who lives four hours away. Since she did not want to drive alone, she decided to take the bus. A reasonable-looking young woman sat down next to her. My wife loves to read, and she was enjoying the trip until the young woman got on her cell phone and had a conversation with a friend. After a few moments, my wife's nonverbal reactions encouraged the young girl to end the call. At the first rest stop, the girl got up and changed seats. For the remainder of the trip, the young woman cradled her phone to her ear like a new mother would hold her child.

Most people would think it offensive if someone listened in on their conversation with another person. Now this situation is reversed. People think it offensive to be forced to listen to someone else's conversation because they talk so loud on their cell phone in public. Fortunately, options are available to deal with the tech asshole. First is to move away from the person, if possible. A similar choice is just to leave. My wife's approach was to use nonverbal communication to show her displeasure and annoyance.

When these efforts are not effective, then one can ask the cell-phone user to take the call later. If the situation is in an office where there is a manager, it is perfectly reasonable to inform the manager. What is not advisable is to take the phone from the person and smash it on the ground. I know it would feel good for a moment. A teacher did that in a classroom, and the aggravation from the parents and the administration was not worth that moment of sheer pleasure. New rule: don't get in trouble over an asshole. There are better things to do with your time.

Lessons Learned

1. *Tech devices distract from relations and an awareness of one's surroundings.*
2. *These mobile devices can be dangerous and devastating to others and ourselves.*
3. *In a group setting, cell phones and other tech tools are an annoyance to others.*

Guided Responses

1. *Log how much time you spend on your devices.*
2. *Is that number high?*
3. *What else could you be doing with those hours?*
4. *Look at the facial responses, gestures, and posture of those around when you are on your devices.*
5. *Be sensitive to those in your company.*
6. *Ask your friends if they think you are addicted.*
7. *Read articles on how to break addictions.*
8. *If guilty, take the first step.*

Activity Sheet

1. **How much time do you spend on your cell phone per day ____ per week ____?**

2. **Estimated number of people who have said you spend too much time on your cell phone ____.**

3. **List by percentage what proportion of time you spend on your phone:**

work	__%
surfing	__%
talking with friends	__%
games	__%
videos	__%
other	__%

4. **What would be a reasonable goal to decrease your use of the cell phone?**

work	__%
surfing	__%
talking with friends	__%
games	__%
videos	__%
other	__%

Juvenile Male Elephants

Young male elephants who were orphaned in the African wild, left the herd, or were relocated without adult elephants, became a menace in Africa's game parks. They would kill rhinos, attack tourist vehicles, destroy property, and make a nuisance of themselves. Park rangers, in an attempt not to kill the young elephants, established a big-brother program for the juvenile males. They placed the juvenile elephants with an adult elephant. Once partnered with an adult, their destructive behavior ceased. When left to themselves, they were obnoxious and dangerous. Like the juvenile male elephants, young people do well with mentors and other adults to help them develop in positive ways.

Nine

Consummate Asshole (CAH)

The Consummate Asshole (CAH) is a person who displays assholeish behavior in most situations. Other authors have identified this type of AH as certified, absolute, undeniable, complete, all-around, or total AH, to mention a few. Some of the CAHs mentioned by these writers are Steve Jobs, Kobe Bryant, Kim Davis, Tom Brady, Carrie Underwood, Rush Limbaugh, Sarah Palin, Kanye West, and Donald Trump. Different writers chose these folks for a variety of reasons, all of which are unflattering and undesirable.

The criteria for choosing the label of Consummate AH rests on the observation that this person is considered an AH by many of those who have contact with CAH. This is not an oops moment, where a person had a hiccup and did this one stupid, disgusting, or demeaning thing to someone else. Rather this is a chosen lifestyle issue. The CAH is self-centered, insensitive to the feelings of others, demeaning to people, and toxic to those who have had to deal with this person.

The terms "certified" and "absolute" were not selected to represent the CAH because those terms might give a mischaracterization of what is meant by CAH. Consummate has the connotation of being masterful, seasoned, accomplished, or complete. As a teacher, I worked for thirteen years with ESE students, who were all diagnosed as severely emotionally disturbed. In order to obtain this diagnosis, classroom teachers, special-education teachers, psychologists, psychiatrists, parents, and administrators evaluated the student. Tests were given, interviews were done, examples were provided, and the history of the student was documented. After all this, these students qualified as ESE students.

This type of objective data gathering is not accumulated to declare someone as a CAH. They are given this designation because most of those around them or those who have to deal with them find their behaviors offensive, annoying, exasperating, and assholeish. Every person has a few of these folks in his or her family, neighborhood, place of work, or social network.

Absolute AH was another term not chosen to define the CAH because no one is entirely bad or evil. There is some good in all of us. Hence, the CAH can at times be polite, charming, or helpful. He or she may be exceptionally talented and can work with others at times toward positive goals. This is another reason for adopting the two AA beliefs: "If one can breathe, there is hope," and "Always leave a door open for someone to change and get well."

As a clergyman, one comment I used to hear from some married couples is that they never had a cross word or thought about their partner. They would sit and smile at me and project this idyllic relationship. However, after listening to them share their experiences together or individually, the real nature of their relationship always came out. They were indeed wonderful, kind, and caring to one another, but they had their moments of irritation and anger with each other.

All couples and relationships have moments of annoyance, exasperation, and anger with one another. So when I say that we all have CAHs in our lives, I know this is true unless the denier is delusional or lying. Either way, it does not make a difference. Everyone has every type of AH in his or her life and needs to deal with them in a constructive manner that does the least amount of damage to himself or herself, the other person, and the relationship.

For self-preservation, most of us spend as little time with the CAH as possible. Unless forced to by work, family, close living proximity, or shared groups, people try to distance themselves from the toxic environment of the CAH. While in the presence of CAHs, people will act civil, polite, and kind for short periods of time until they can make their escape. The use of the skills mentioned in chapter two will help make this time bearable. Whatever our relation to the CAH, there is the need to think thoroughly how one is going to interact with this person.

The following is a case study I was involved with that contains both good and poor examples of how to deal with the CAH. Using fictitious names, Shirley will represent the CAH, and Betty will represent her counterpart. While these two women were both board members in the same club, they were casual acquaintances at best, with no prior tension between them.

In a closed community setting, many knew Shirley as a CAH. She would lie, exaggerate stories, make offensive comments about others, and give misleading information. She was a general sour presence in groups. Shirley had a part-time job but was fired for lying to the owner and other staff. People avoided partnering with Shirley because of her negativity, posturing, and annoying behavior.

One evening, Shirley, Betty, and four other board members were meeting to discuss the club's business. At one point in the discussion, Betty made a point about a situation the group had been dealing with for over a year. Betty's position was consistent from the beginning. Shirley repeatedly challenged her, saying Betty had changed her position because it now benefited her in some obscure way.

Betty objected and cited examples of her early position, which was consistent with her present policy. It was obvious to all that Betty was accurate and Shirley was being irritating. Instead of this minor argument ending with Betty saying, "OK, let's move on," Betty, who was experiencing a number of personal challenges in her life, said, "Shirley, you are just a liar."

And Betty got up, excused herself, and left the room. The stunned group fell into an awkward silence. A few days later, Betty approached Shirley privately and apologized for the outburst. Shirley would have none of it and told Betty she would have nothing to do with her ever again. Because the two would continue as board members, Shirley told Betty she would ignore her and asked Betty not to speak to her. A few weeks later, Betty again tried to apologize for the outburst, and once more, Shirley rebuffed her.

The importance of this event is that it has continuing consequences for Betty, Shirley, the other board members, and the group. When both women are at the same event, there is a loss of freedom as they awkwardly tiptoe around each other.

What went wrong, and what can be learned from this case study? Before analyzing the case, a reminder of the third premise of the book from chapter one is helpful. Start with high expectations and develop the best possible outcome. Then implement the strategies and tools to accomplish that goal. Next, ask if this goal is possible or if it is worth the effort. When the most desired goal does not materialize, then work down the scale to get the best BATNA possible.

In this case, Betty was remorseful for her part in the incident. She wanted to restore the relationship to friendly terms and took the steps she felt necessary to mend the relationship. That obviously did not work out, so she had to take the best outcome she could get, which was very low on her desired list. In dealing with difficult people and situations, it is always good to be proactive and prepared for what could happen.

Unfortunately the situation around the table did not lend itself to being proactive or prepared, and this is how many bad encounters happen. Someone injects something that is not on the agenda or is negative or blaming, and conflict instantly arises. One person can't predict what the other individual is going to say or do; however, each person is responsible for his or her response and the resulting consequences.

Betty heard something that was untrue about her, and she was offended. It is true that she was going through some difficult personal challenges and she was edgy. However, everyone has trying moments, and the burden is on that individual to deal with the pressure in a healthy and nondestructive manner. This being the case, Betty needed to recognize that she was under pressure, sensitive, and vulnerable. Feeling the irritation and then anger well up in her, she should have caught herself and done a quick mental and emotional inventory.

She should have asked herself, *Am I in a good place to deal with this? Should I excuse myself from the situation? How can I frame this or address this to get at a truer picture of the situation? How can I respond without blowing up the place?*

Everyone has had a cold or illness and needed a day off from work. This does not show weakness, lack of courage, or determination to hang in there. Rather it is a wise course of action in order to get well and not spread the cold to others. It is the same in social encounters when under a great deal of stress. This is not the time to address some situations. Take a break and come back to it another day when the pressures and tension have passed.

Betty could have said, "This is not correct, but I am not in a good place to deal with it right now. Please excuse me."

And then she could have left. Taking a breather from the incident and thinking more about the situation, she may later decide the issue is not worth pursuing because everyone knew Shirley was just being an asshole.

Another response she could have used was to go to Shirley later and explain her position, trusting Shirley would see her error and have the conflict end. If an understanding could not be reached, Betty could have left it as a difference of opinion and moved on.

However, it is perfectly legitimate for a person to stay and address the conflict. If Betty were in a better frame of mind, she could have taken several deep breaths and cited more information to prove her point, or she could have asked the group its opinion since most knew the situation and would have supported her.

Regrettably Betty did not choose one of those options, but she fired something off that, though correct, was very hurtful and had long-term consequences.

The original exchange happened, and there is no taking it back. Could anything be done after to repair the damage? Betty, to the best of her ability, reached out twice to try to make amends. The gestures were rejected outright, leaving them both in an ill-at-ease relationship that affects not only both of them but also others in the group who have to deal with both women.

Even though this type of encounter happens quickly, it is wise to check oneself. Ask yourself, "What do I want from this relationship?" With a person whom Betty has had a long history of conflict, she may have decided enough is enough and drew her line in the sand. Betty could have continued to argue her case, citing more evidence; involve others; and confront Shirley on her history of false stories.

At this point, it is nasty, but there is some benefit. First, the issue has been put on the table. Shirley has been put on notice that her exaggerations, misspoken statements, and lies will be challenged in the future. Shirley may think twice before going down that road again, at least with Betty. When pushed, bullies and AHs will respect someone who stands up for himself or herself.

Some things about this case were handled well, while others were dealt with poorly. Appropriating good communication skills could have avoided the poisoned environment that resulted. The case also demonstrates that even using appropriate strategies, such as attempting to make amends, does not always work. The actors themselves always determine the end results.

Lessons Learned

1. *Allow yourself to feel the situation.*
2. *Do not allow the feelings or the moment to overtake you.*
3. *Give yourself breathing room to deal with the encounter. Walk away if time is not right.*
4. *If you choose to stay and confront, consider the consequences.*
5. *Use your communication skills and problem-solving strategies.*
6. *Apologize for any of your shortcomings in the affair.*
7. *Do not apologize for others' actions. Allow the offending party*
8. *the opportunity to own what they did.*

Guided Responses

1. *What triggers your emotional flare-ups? What words, topics, events, or people bring on anger or anxiety?*
2. *Think through what skills or strategies to use in order to manage your emotions.*
3. *Plan a response that will be helpful for you.*

Activity Sheet

1. What are your triggers (something that sets off extreme anxiety or anger in a person)?

	Words	Actions	People
Home			
Work			
Social Settings			

2. Think of an encounter with a CAH that did not turn out well.

a. What did you say?

____

____

b. What did the other person say?

____

____

3. **From chapter two, which skills could have made this encounter a win-win: active listening, "I messages," or problem solving?**

    ____

    ____

4. **Write out specifically how you would restate your response.**

    ____

    ____

5. **Repeat questions two through four for other situations that did not turn out well.**

6. **Write out a response for your trigger situations to prepare you for the next encounter with a CAH.**

Walrus

This hefty mammal may be the clumsiest animal on the planet. It weighs twenty-two hundred pounds with a seemly disproportionately small head, no ears, and two tusks. It spends a third of its life on rocks or ice floes, and it has only flippers and no legs to move around. The walrus uses its flippers to waddle and lumber its way to thrust itself on the rocks. Their combat is the most uncoordinated and clumsy display in nature. They crash up against one another with their massive layers of blubber and try to knock each other with their small heads. They can't help who they are and seem to enjoy the company of one another while lying on the rocks. We are who we are, so the trick is to look at our good qualities, appreciate them, be content, and keep moving in a positive direction.

Ten

Awkward Asshole (AAH)

This type of AH to be defined and discussed was purposely left to the end because it is significantly different from the others.

"Withitness" (with-it-ness) is a term that educators use to describe a teacher who knows what is going on in the classroom. This includes who is not paying attention, who is distracting others, who is texting messages on his or her phone, who is not understanding, and who needs special help. The term is commonly understood as having "eyes in the back of one's head." This is one of the most critical components of a teacher's skill set because it helps maintain order so students can learn. A teacher or aide who lacks withitness contributes to misbehavior, unruliness, and lack of learning in the classroom.

Withitness, though not stated as withitness outside educational circles, is prevalent in every aspect of people's lives to include families, friends, acquaintances, work, and recreation. People gravitate toward those with withitness. Folks with withitness are easy to talk to and be around because they develop a mutual rhythm with others, establish an easy ebb and flow to conversation, and are able to find common ground and understanding with others. Their association and involvement in relationships seems effortless.

On the other side of the coin, there are those who, because of their awkwardness, are difficult to be around. These folks are awkward in their ability to understand a situation without explanation. They find it difficult to say what they mean or want. Their timing is off in conversations, and their social skills are cumbersome, usually disrupting the flow of interaction among individuals and groups. In spite of their awkwardness, these folks may be bright, capable, good workers and employees. They are friendly and can be an asset to the community in every way. They are just awkward.

Are these awkward folks assholes? Some say yes because they slow down progress; others get tired of explaining things to them. They interrupt at inconvenient times, say inappropriate things, and generally make people feel uncomfortable. I have heard fellow participants say about a fellow worker responsible for getting information out to their group, "I just can't take the slowness of that asshole any longer." They excuse themselves to take a walk or get a coffee before coming back and trying to finish the task. The awkward person can be the nicest, most sensitive, well-intended, gracious, and respectful person on the team. Are they an AH? In my opinion, at this point, no, they are not. In others' calculations, yes, they are.

To me, these folks are just awkward but are out of step with others. The awkward person just can't help how his or her DNA is wired. By my calculation, being awkward alone does not make a person an AH. This individual lives with his or her awkwardness as those with learning disabilities live with their afflictions. However, it is also true that anyone, including an awkward person, can be an AH in the right circumstances if he or she is displaying assholeish behavior.

When I was a clergyman, a young gifted person in our church was awkward. It was frustrating to talk with him because I always thought we were on different pages trying to communicate. Around and around we would go because he knew what he wanted but had a difficult time explaining it, even though he was a bright person. It took most of my communication skills to keep him focused enough to unravel his thoughts. Many of the church members had the same problem with this parishioner. He had an excellent mind and eye for detail, and his comments were usually helpful. If one made the effort to hear him, he had pearls of wisdom to share.

He was awkward, but at times he drifted into the AH category. Like a few others in the church, he had ideas about what the church should be doing. He thought it the responsibility of the church to rise to the task of doing whatever he thought should be done. His reasoning went like this. "Pastor, God has given me a vision that the church should be creating a safe place for runaways in our community." He would then explain in an unconventional manner what should be done, who should do it, how it should be executed, and how it could be financed. This was all worked out in his head, but it would take forever to get it all out.

However, when he insisted our church do this work, conflict arose. Once his mind was made up, he believed it was my responsibility to make it happen as a leader of the church. Judgment and implied condemnation followed if he did not get his way. The inflexible insistence took an inordinate amount of time and became a pain in the neck.

While this example is in a religious context, the principles are easily transferred to nonreligious settings. My AAH parishioner claimed that God led him to speak about this new work, and he was expecting the church to get to it and get it done. In his mind, since I was the head of the church, it was my responsibility to get the task done. As the minister of the church, I told him his idea was a worthwhile work. Since God had put this to him, he should continue to follow it up by writing a proposal to the board, explaining the idea and how it could be done. This should include time allotment, money needed, any other resources, the number of people required, an outlined management structure, scheduling, and any other information that could help the board make a proper decision.

He was insistent that I do this as head of the church. It was my job, he claimed. Finally, I told him that I did not hear God calling me to do this. However, my support was fully behind the effort if he wanted to continue and make this plan a reality. He claimed not to know how to do this, which was not true, because he had already explained it to me. I encouraged him to talk with others and see if anyone could be found to take on the task. This new work never materialized, and he continued to blame me for its failure.

One of the first things a person learns when moving into a fifty-five or older community is not to ask, "How are you?" Almost everyone in this community has had at least one surgery and suffers from multiple aches and pains. Since you don't want to give opportunity for someone to go on and on about his or her ailments, you learn to ask these types of questions: Did you go to the show last night? What is the weather to be like today? What are your plans for the weekend?

An acquaintance of mine, who would never win the withitness award, gave a sad and revolting display of lacking this character trait. A woman was sharing that her father developed dementia, along with other medical issues, and had come to the point where he could not live alone. Because of financial reasons, she and her sibling took the responsibility to care for him in their homes. The father was vocally abusive, incontinent, and demanding and needed twenty-four-hour care. This act of love became a real burden on the family.

While she was explaining the situation to me, she was almost in tears. I tried to offer some comfort by telling her of my experience in caring for my father before he passed. I shared with how difficult the task was but how rewarding it was at the end. She, clearly distraught, continued to share her heartache for her father.

Another person who was a part of the conversation said, "Well, that's what you get with Obamacare!"

Should the elephant in the room be addressed? Yes, he is awkward. Yes, he has no withitness. Is he an asshole? Some would say no. Watching the expression on my friend's face, I say, in this instance, yes, he is an asshole. We both chose to ignore his comment. It was one of the few times I wanted to spank an adult.

At the end of the day, most awkward people are just awkward and need a little time and patience from others. They are capable people who can make a wonderful contribution if given the chance. The use of a well-placed look of disapproval to the AAH is helpful for him or her to see that his or her comment or action is not appropriate.

Lessons Learned

1. *Recognize the contribution of others.*
2. *Give time and use skills to help others unlock their thoughts.*
3. *Serious conversations deserve serious contributions, not jokes.*
4. *Well-placed gestures can help others realize appropriate and inappropriate responses.*

Guided Responses

1. *Take a moment and try to understand and read a situation.*
2. *Follow the lead of others.*

Activity Sheet

1. **Think of a situation when dealing with an awkward person. What active listening, assertive, or problem-solving skills could help the situation?**

2. **Write out three different ways you could frame a response to help the communication process.**

   a. ____________________

   ____

   b. ____________________

   ____

   c. ____________________

   ____

African Lion

This majestic beast with his flowing mane is known as the king of the jungle. The lion is born with all the advantages to be king. He is blessed with power, strength, and speed to defeat almost all other creatures. While he rules his domain, the lion is brutally cruel to the weakest in his pride. When a male lion becomes the new leader of the pride, he kills off all the male cubs so he can mate with the females. It works for him but is deadly to the others, especially the young and defenseless. Humans create cultural mores that guide behavior and establish laws that protect our weakest members. We create charitable organizations that help protect the widows, the orphans, the homeless, the weak, and the damaged.

Eleven

Exceptional Asshole (EAH)

In everyone's life, there is an exceptional AH, that person who is head and shoulders above everyone else in your life to claim the prize as the biggest asshole you know. This could be a family member, in-law, friend, neighbor, coworker, employer, politician, or anyone who has affected you the most with his or her assholeish behavior.

After rewinding my life's movie and considering all those who have disgusted me, two choices emerged. One choice is a person I have known and interacted with for years. Just thinking about this person brings me down and ties my stomach in a knot. No matter what is said to this person in an encouraging, loving fashion or outright heated confrontation regarding his abuse, selfishness, neglect, and just plain all-around assholeishness, he just goes on his merry way, oblivious to the hurt he smears on those around him. His impact is local and confined to family, a few friends, fellow workers, neighbors, and acquaintances.

The winner for my "Exceptional Asshole" is someone who I have never met, but he turns my stomach whenever I hear his voice or see his face. My Exceptional Asshole is Donald Trump. He so far outdistances any assholes I have known that he deserves a soft round of applause for being the "biglyest" asshole in my life.

In my world, a decent man does not

- walk into teenage girls' dressing rooms when some are without clothes, sneak a peek, and then brag about it to the world;
- talk about women's menstrual cycles in order to embarrass them;
- objectify women;
- grab women by their private body parts and brag about it;
- say a woman is so unattractive that he would never sexually abuse her;
- accuse a woman of adultery without a single piece of evidence;
- call women ugly;
- advocate violence towards women; or
- brag about his daughter's body parts.

In my world, a grown man does not talk about desiring a fifteen-year-old girl. In my world, a father does not insinuate he would like to have relations with his daughter. Not in my world. These are just some of the things the Donald has done or said publicly to shame women.

This is just the tip of the iceberg. Take a moment and think about all the groups and people this man has insulted and shamed publicly. Though not exhaustive, the list includes immigrants, Mexicans, working people, billionaires, the poor, African Americans, Latinos, Jews, Muslims, Christians, mothers and their babies, military officers, veterans, families of our fallen soldiers, America's allies, the press, foreigners, veterans, prisoners of war, academicians, conservationists, workers who don't have wealthy parents to bail them out, contractors, subcontractors, honest folks, and decent people everywhere who don't appreciate or tolerate his vulgarity or condemnation.

So what can be done with an asshole who attacks the very core of decency, decorum, and democracy that honorable people treasure? What can really be done? How do decent people defend themselves against The Donald with his wealth, his power, his surrogates, and people of his ilk?

As of this writing, Trump has demonstrated an affinity for Russia, and it is from the Russians that lessons can be learned. Yes, even from the most ruthless and violent Russian, Joseph Stalin, we can learn. On July 28, 1942,

Joseph Stalin issued Order No. 227 that called for Russian resistance against Germany. A line that became famous in the order is, "Not one step back!" This has become a rallying cry to stand against evil and never retreat. Stalin's instruction is helpful because it calls for people to know what is important and what they stand for and not to take "one step backward" from decency and honesty.

The first step in dealing with Trump or someone like him is to deal with yourself. Know yourself. Know what your core values are. Know what you believe. Know what you really stand for. Once you know what you stand for, then you know what to stand against. This understanding will direct you on when, why, and how to use communication skills. These skills are the first line of defense and the first step to any offense. These skills can be implemented anywhere, anytime, and with anyone. In every conversation with others, these skills are one's tools for standing for decency and confronting the vileness and corruption that is ripping the heart and soul out of our country and its people.

Once a person understands his or her core values, this person will find ways—and there are so many different ways—to confront and defeat assholes, no matter what their position is.

Lessons Learned

1. *Set your values high.*
2. *Follow your values, and don't let fame, fortune, or intimidation distract you.*
3. *Speak for decency and honesty.*
4. *Don't take one step backward.*

Guided Responses

1. *Don't accept, tolerate, or give in to assholeish behavior.*
2. *Challenge AH behavior in all ways possible.*
3. *Use communication skills and problem-solving strategies to defend against the EAH and to confront the EAH.*

Activity Sheet

1. **Using the three-part "I message," write out statements to confront the behavior of an AH.**
   a. ______________________________

   ____

   b. ______________________________

   ____

   c. ______________________________

   ____

2. **List other ways besides direct confrontation to deal with AH behavior.**
   a. ______________________________
   b. ______________________________
   c. ______________________________
   d. ______________________________
   e. ______________________________

3. **Write out a plan of action to deal with AHs.**

Conclusion

What is your life worth? It is your life.

When teaching my classes at school, I would ask the question, "What can't people take from you?" There would be a number of answers, and discussion would follow. It was easy to see that possessions can be stolen or destroyed, money can be lost, friendships dissolved, and even family members can turn upon one another.

One answer commonly given by students was a person's reputation can't be taken from him or her. They argued that no one could take your reputation because if you accomplished something and people knew you had done that, then your reputation would always be intact. A counter to that proposition was, "What if you were accused of cheating and people said that you didn't deserve the credit for your accomplishments? Even if the accusation were false, your reputation would be tarnished, so it *can* be taken from you." History can be rewritten, records expunged, and people forget.

Usually a student will say, "Yes, but if you know you did not cheat, they can't take away the fact that you know you did not cheat." Bingo, this student gets an A+. No one can take away what you know to be true about yourself. They can take everything else, but not what is inside you.

Self-worth is what no can take from you. It is not your worth as the world records worth. It is your self-worth. You know you have acted honorably, been fair, helped others, and done the right thing, and you were honest in dealing with others. People can make up lies and run your name into the ground, but you know you, and your self-worth remains intact. No one can take your self-worth from you, and you should always be mindful of your self-worth.

In summary, how are AHs managed?

1. Know yourself and your self-worth. No one can take that from you, and from this, all decisions and actions are made.
2. Deal with yourself first. Recognize the assholeishness in you, and deal with it. Be aware of what triggers you to be an AH. No one is perfect, but we can all choose to get better inch by inch. Confront yourself, or

someone else will confront you. Develop the desire not to be an AH. Wake up every morning and commit to doing the right thing.

3. Learn healthy strategies and techniques to deal with others, and use them.
4. Adopt quality premises to live by. The ones given in the book are a start. Anyone who is breathing has a chance. Always be willing to help, and leave an open door so the person can take a first step to getting well. Respect the other person. You have to deal with the assholes in your world, but you do not have to be dragged down to their level. Set boundaries on how you will help. Support others who are doing the right thing. Stand your ground, and confront dishonesty and injustice. Take care of yourself.
5. Expect adversity, distractions, and insults. And then deal with them.
6. Take the time needed to make the right decision. Just say, "I am sorry, but I need time to think about that."
7. Think about what you really want in a situation. Be careful with this one, and then go for it.

How do you want to leave this world? Most of the time, we do not choose the time, place, or method of how we will pass from this earth. We do have a choice on whether we leave honorably or not. Every day we make the choice to act honorably or not. Our communication and life skills will help us make honorable decisions, which will follow us when we pass on.

No one is perfect, and anyone can change. On April 20, 2015, a firing squad in an Indonesian prison shot eight prisoners to death. All were convicted of drug trafficking. The prisoners were from Australia, Brazil, Ghana, and Indonesia. While incarcerated, they found faith. They made a decision to change. As they were staked to poles waiting to be shot, they began to sing the song "Amazing Grace." They sang until they were shot to death.

Amazing grace, How sweet the sound
That saved a wretch like me
I once was lost, but now I'm found
T'was blind, but now I see

'Twas grace that taught my heart to fear
And grace my fears relieved
How precious did that grace appear
The hour I first believed

Through many dangers, toils and snares
We have already come
T'was grace that brought us safe thus far
And grace will lead us home.

As long as we have a breath, we have a chance to better ourselves. Take the opportunity left to you and commit to making your life less stressful, more gratifying and more fulfilling.

What does your heart mean?

About the Author

Philip Edwards is a Vietnam veteran and urban specialist whose work has brought him everywhere from Chicago to Nairobi, Kenya.

While pastoring urban churches, Edwards led his congregations to reach out to marginalized groups such as sex trade workers, addicts, the homeless, and street gangs. During that time, he counselled families in crisis and taught courses in communication skills and problem solving. Later, he worked as a mediator in the provincial courts of Ontario and as a teacher for the severely emotionally disturbed.

He hopes that readers of his book will learn new skills and strengthen their existing skills in navigating life's daily challenges. Edwards also writes a monthly historical column for his local newspaper. His writings can be accessed at chooserightly.com.

Made in the USA
Columbia, SC
10 December 2020

27303533R00072